Stardust
and
Ashes

Stardust
and
Ashes

*Science fiction in
Christian perspective*

Stephen May

First published in Great Britain 1998
Society for Promoting Christian Knowledge
Holy Trinity Church
Marylebone Road
London NW1 4DU

All Scripture quotations in this book are from the Revised Standard
Version of the Bible, copyrighted 1973 by the Division of
Christian Education of the National Council of the Churches
of Christ in the USA.

British Library Cataloguing-in-Publication Data
A catalogue record of this book is available
from the British Library

ISBN 0–281–05104–6

Typeset by Pioneer Associates, Perthshire
Printed in Great Britain by
The Cromwell Press, Melksham, Wiltshire

Contents

Acknowledgements

I am grateful for the encouragement and suggestions of a whole host of friends and teachers over the years. I recall particularly Nigel Mathers, Nick Wilson, Paul May, Chris Dunton, Bill Beattie, Elliot Wardlaw, Sally Stone, James and Alan Torrance, Bob Walker, Nick Parish, Pete Whittaker, Leslie Turfrey, Graham Redding, Jeremy Law, Graham Hamilton, Andrew Doubleday, Hamish Thomson, Andrew Burgess, Doug Campbell and Craig Forbes. I beg the forgiveness of any inadvertently omitted. Some of the ideas have been tried out at St John's College, Auckland (notably in the 'science fiction and theology group'), the Bible College of New Zealand, the University of Otago and King's College, London.

Various sections of this book have been written in New Zealand, Tonga, Oxford and Cambridge, notably on sabbatical from St John's College, Auckland, whose Dean and Governors have supported this endeavour. Les Brighton, Francis Foulkes, Lance Stone and Lawrence Osborn have been remarkably generous of their time, and Dr Harold and Mrs Maud Turner of the use of a room in their house. For the actual publishing of this book, I am especially appreciative of the support and tolerant encouragement of Dr Andrew Walker and that of my editors Naomi Starkey and Alison Lawson, whose patience has been Joblike and advice Solomonic. My use of the VCR has prevented my children, Jenny and Peter, from watching as many episodes of *Playschool* as they might have liked. To College typists Jill Bartlett and Lois Anderson, hearty thanks too.

Finally, to my wife Marion I owe the greatest debt of

thanks. She has supported me in all ways in this apparently interminable project; putting up with a vast collection of videos and books. She has read innumerable drafts, encouraged continually and maintained a fierce optimism about the prospect of actually completing this project. To her I owe that, as so much else.

STEPHEN MAY

*To my father whose store of science fiction
magazines in the attic sent me on this journey.*

*To my dearest wife, Marion, whose patience
endured whilst I explored it.*

———

Earth to earth, ashes to ashes, dust to dust:
In sure and certain hope of the Resurrection to
    eternal life,
through our Lord Jesus Christ.

(The Book of Common Prayer, 1662)

Introduction

One of the most striking things about culture in the 1980s and 1990s has been the growth of science fiction. Its iconography has spread everywhere, from cereal packets to dessert advertising. In the cinema, the great blockbusters that drag in massive audiences have increasingly become science-fiction epics. As far back as January 1984 the top four money-making films in history were science fiction films – and that was before *Jurassic Park* (1993) and *Independence Day* (1996).[1] The language of space-travel, light-years, hyperspace and so forth has become common currency to the modern generation. Pop lyrics are full of extra-terrestrials, starships and the like. At the other end of the spectrum, even operas have been written on science fiction themes.[2] What was regarded twenty years ago as an amiable eccentricity has become the norm of modern culture, fed repetitively on images of men floating free in space above the rotating earth, of lunar rangers bumping over the cratered moon's surface, of spectacular views from interplanetary probes of Jupiter's moons or Halley's comet. Films like *2001: A Space Odyssey* (1968) were paralleled even as they returned to the cinemas and television by the massively publicized space shots of the competing nations. In 1986 the spectacularly disastrous explosion of the space shuttle *Challenger* brought a crisis in American self-confidence, inducing President Reagan to say that the nation's heroes had 'slipped the surly bonds of earth . . . and touched the face of God'.[3] This awareness has not even been a Western one, for all that it is powered by Western technology and ideology: a Nigerian novelist, writing of his experiences in the Biafran war almost thirty years ago,

1

records how he spent his time in a prison, perhaps expecting death, working out the script of a science fiction novel.[4]

How are we to regard this characteristic phenomenon of our age, this most modern expansion of our horizons? It used to be argued that the sight of the Earth from space would relativize human problems, would show us how trivial our differences are, that we are all bound together on 'Spaceship Earth'. How far this vision has failed to sustain itself is easy to see. It is nevertheless a characteristic of science fiction, and of its associated worldview (which is even now spreading its tentacles throughout our modern civilization) to speak of 'Man' – the male term being typical. Speech is not so much of 'the Americans on the Moon' as 'Man's' arrival there: 'one small step for a man; one giant leap for mankind' as Neil Armstrong meant to say. Newspaper articles write of the future in terms of 'Man's' arrival on Mars, the development of colonies in space, the necessity of government investment in space research. This growth in confidence about expanding horizons seems matched in some quarters by intensified despair about 'the Old World'. Science fiction novels seem to assume the necessity of escaping Earth before its inhabitants succeed in finally destroying it – and this too is a symptom of the modern age, of a world which has awoken to the threat of nuclear devastation, amplified now by the terrifying scenarios of 'nuclear winter'.

The modern world is one of staggering change (a mode of existence that is the very subject matter of science fiction), bringing the possibility of both excitement and terror. Ours is the most affluent society ever known on Earth, and it is also the only one apparently capable of bringing itself to an abrupt end in a matter of weeks or months. The Black Death is estimated to have killed up to one-third to one-half of the population of parts of Europe over a period of years in the fourteenth century – one of the worst catastrophes ever suffered by the human race. What nuclear war (and its associated chemical and biological counterparts, along with famine, plague, and so forth) threaten, is unimaginably worse, so much so, that – as is obvious – most people prefer not to think about it for too long. Science fiction, within its own criteria, has discussed matters such as these during the whole period of its history. It may not be, as a leading science fiction writer has described it, 'the characteristic art form of the twentieth century',[5] let alone, according to an even more grandiose claim, 'the only literary form which concerns itself with reality',[6] but it is certainly not one that can be ignored with any comfort. Doris Lessing has even described it as 'the most original branch of literature now',[7] Stephen Clark as 'our century's greatest gift to literature'.[8]

This question of the literary value of science fiction (or sf – never that film reviewers' abomination, 'sci-fi') is one that I shall look at later in this work. For my purposes here, however, the primary issue is that of the cultural significance of science fiction. The news that four times as many people in Britain watch repeats of *Star Trek* on television as go to church on Sunday attracted the attention of the Anglican weekly the *Church Times*,[9] as did a report that a Spanish linguist has translated the Bible into Klingon. It is estimated that 15–20 per cent of the fiction now published annually in the USA is science fiction. It is clear that, whilst sf may still be regarded by some as trash, it is, at the very least, widespread and influential.

It is the argument of this book, however, that science fiction is not *just* a popular phenomenon (and worthy of being looked at for that reason alone); it is a popular phenomenon that embodies many of the cultural assumptions of our age. Sf embodies in its 'myths' our age's characteristic worldview – on the origin of humanity, its nature, destiny and relationship to the wider universe.

Whilst the content of those myths is significant, though, so too is the form. Science fiction is *fiction*.[10] In sf, anything goes. The 'space' given by the genre to sheer play gives it more than half its intoxication. 'Don't dullify it', pleaded Frank Herbert, the author of *Dune* (1965).[11] At the heart of sf is enjoyment, delight in possibility. Some have wanted to rename sf 'speculative fiction'. A number of responses to this central aspect of imaginative delight are available: one is celebration!

How does one respond to this as a Christian? I believe that not only is science fiction to be taken seriously as an expression of modern culture, but the issues with which it deals are also not to be despised. If, as Christians hold, God took us humans so seriously that he became one of us in the incarnation, we cannot adopt a sniffy attitude to modern culture. The carol says 'he did not abhor the Virgin's womb', and neither must we abhor anything either. Early Christian theologians too had a saying: God became what we are so that we might become like him. This (the pattern of the incarnation) is binding on all Christians. It means those who follow Christ must engage with the culture that surrounds them – and of which they are a part more than they think. Christians need to avoid the snobbish attitude to popular culture which looks down on it from a tremendous height, one that puts Jane Austen and Isaac Asimov in two totally different caskets.

It is not just Christians who can have this kind of attitude. Sf critic Darko Suvin describes sf as a kind of 'paraliterature', but with no reason to be snubbed for all that.[12] Christians have even more reason to listen to 'paraliterature' than most. As Erich Auerbach's classic work of literary criticism, *Mimesis* shows,[13] Christianity was regarded as a vulgar religion in the ancient world, one suitable only for women and slaves. Its own Scriptures were written in common *koine* Greek. Four centuries later, Saint Augustine struggled with taunts from educated pagans about the Gospels' unsophisticated style. In the Middle Ages, Mystery Plays and the like brought Christianity to the masses at the most crude and ribald level. It is only in comparatively recent times that Christianity and high art have become bedfellows.

I hope that sf fans who are not Christians (it is possible to be both!) will recognize in this book a fair and accurate portrayal of the genre they love. I also (obviously) hope they might be led further. As people who pride themselves on openness to new possibilities, I challenge them to at least have a good think about the questions it raises – rather than dismissing them out of hand! As can be seen, this book has grown out of a my own interest in both science fiction and Christianity and conviction of their importance. I was, and am, a science fiction fan, yet I am also a professional theologian. Yet, whilst my perspective has altered, I still read and watch sf for fun.

Some regard a taste for sf as a sign, as literary critic John Wain once remarked, of 'intellectual bankruptcy';[14] others – more charitably – as a tolerable weakness, evident at least of humanity. What is said in the pages that follow is written as much to me as to anyone else. It is the result of a long dialogue with science fiction.

A luridly covered novel of space and time which I remember carrying about school around the age of thirteen symbolized the early appeal of sf to me. In the mould of Jack Williamson or A. E. Van Vogt or Edmond Hamilton, it depicted a man caught up out of the twentieth century and projected (I have forgotten how) thousands of years into the future, into a time of interstellar war. The scope was enormous both in space and time; all the classical, Aristotelian 'unities' were broken. Although its author is now forgotten, the 'feel' of it is intense to this day. So too the exotic marvels of the 1964 films *The First Men in the Moon* and *Robinson Crusoe on Mars* which I saw at the local (now demolished) cinema around the same time. They played fast and loose with their originals, but that was lost on me. What I vividly recall are their grasp of the 'sense of wonder', alienness, the feeling of being lost in a strange, new world of colour, gorgeousness and marvels not to be imagined.

Something remains to be said about my cultural perceptions. This book was written in New Zealand, Oxford and even Tonga. The last parts found formulation in Cambridge, a matter of yards from the Cavendish Laboratory where Crick and Watson discovered the structure of DNA in 1953 and Ernest Rutherford split the atom in 1919. It was a good place to finish, the site to which James Clerk Maxwell came as its first professor. He was the man acknowledged by Einstein to be fundamental for the break with classical Newtonian physics and also a devout Christian who saw no conflict between his faith and rigorous inquiry into God's world. For me, he is a model of Christian activity.

New Zealand, the country where I live myself, tends to think of itself as isolated, free from the threat of nuclear holocaust which still hangs over the rest of the world like a Damocles' sword, not as terrifying as in my youth but still there. Yet New Zealand is aware of ecological threats – the growing ozone hole over the South Pole, increasing rates of skin cancer, the destruction of marine life in the South Pacific from unregulated or illegal fishing, the pollution of waters from French nuclear testing at Muroroa Atoll, the fear of global warming from the Greenhouse effect, leading to rising sea levels and the drowning of low Pacific atolls. It is still part of 'Spaceship Earth', part of the global village. A nuclear war might not affect it as badly as other countries, but it would be hurt, even if the winds carrying nuclear fallout were kind.

Against the winds of intellectual change, however, there is no defence.[15] The modern Western mindset has spread wide, blowing throughout the world, its fallout lying unnoticed perhaps but conditioning and changing. Sf expresses the myths of that outlook; it is about those that this book is concerned.

Chapter 1

The vast abyss of night

A dream of stars

When we go out at night and look up at the stars, we are looking back in time. Perhaps it is the only time-machine we will ever have – contrary to the thoughts of some science fiction writers. The light that reaches us has set out years before on that journey, many hundreds, thousands or even millions of years previously. The age of our universe is now generally accepted to be somewhere around 10 to 15 billion (10,000 to 15,000 million) years[1] and – if we could see far enough – we would see the light coming from that first big explosion – the 'Big Bang', as it is conventionally called. The astronomers *can* see this, not with their visible eyes but with machines that measure other frequencies of the electromagnetic spectrum of which visible light is merely one part (at one end are gamma-rays, at the other radio waves). Astronomers can detect the microwave radiation of 3 degrees above absolute zero (minus 270 degrees centigrade) that indicates the beginning of the universe: this background radiation dates from a 'mere' million years after the 'Big Bang'.[2]

We, obviously, cannot do this. But we can see a long, long way. The constellation Orion that is easily recognizable by most people in both hemispheres is dominated by two bright stars, Betelgeuse and Rigel. Of these, Betelgeuse is a mere 300 light-years away, Rigel slightly further away at 900 light-years. Other gas clouds in the constellation Orion are even further away.[3] These are small distances in astronomical terms but – for us at least – they are by no means insignificant. A light-year is the distance light travels in a year at a

constant, unalterable velocity of 186,000 miles per second.
The light that reaches us now from the star Rigel set out
from that star 900 years ago. What is the state of that star
now? We cannot know. Perhaps it is blowing up? If so, we
will not be aware of this – only our descendants living on
Earth in 900 years' time will know (if there are humans on
Earth in 900 years' time!). Even the light we receive from
our sun has taken 8¼ minutes to reach us.

The nearest major galaxy to our own (what we call the
Milky Way, that dim cascade of stars across the zenith) is
the Andromeda Nebula, M31. It is two million light years
away, so that the awesome view of Andromeda we see in
photographs is actually two million years out of date.

This vastness of the universe is staggering. I remember
learning at school that the horizon is some 14 miles distant
on earth because of the curvature of our planet. If we climb
a high hill we can see further. On high places like the Puy-
de-Dôme in the Massif Central in France, we often find
stones and markers set to indicate far objects, maybe up to
20, 50 or even 100 miles away. But when we are looking into
space we are looking infinitely further and for that all we
have to do is to step outside when it is dark and look up. And
there we see the universe in all its glory.

This sense is, I believe, the emotional heart of science
fiction. This is the centre of *Star Trek* (1966), of *Star Wars*
(1977), *Close Encounters of the Third Kind* (1977) – the stars
rushing past, the two suns in the sky, the enormous mother-
ship settling over Devil's Tower in Wyoming. What if there
are things 'out there'? Maybe other beings like ourselves?
The universe is so vast, how can we know? The scientists tell
us of the millions of suns elsewhere even in our domestic
galaxy (which is a hundred thousand light-years in diameter);
surely, we think, some must have planets and – given that
plurality – must not many too have developed life, have
intelligent beings like us who wonder: 'Is there anything out
there?'

Science fiction has always rejoiced in the image of space
travel – first journeys to the moon, interplanetary colonization of Mars, economic exploitation of the asteroids, perhaps
trips to Venus, the Jovian satellites and so forth; then the first

interstellar flights, powered either by newly discovered FTL (faster than light) breakthrough technology that conveniently enables humanity to avoid the limiting barrier of the speed of light or 'sublight' generation starships taking maybe centuries to reach the nearest stars. After that, the galaxies are our oyster!

Actual science is somewhat more prosaic. The vastly expensive American space programme in the 1960s – fuelled by intense political rivalry with the Soviet Union – put astronauts on the moon within a decade – as John Kennedy had promised. After that funding dried up, being put back into 'Star Wars' (SDI) and other aspects of the military-industrial complex. Unxpected complications, cost over-runs and the disastrous *Challenger* explosion of 1986 held up the Shuttle project and the space programme with it. The so-called benefits of investment in space have so far proved illusory. Indeed, it looks now not as if the space age is just beginning but that it has already ended.[4] No country can justify the huge expense needed with present technology to escape the earth's 'gravity well' – interplanetary travel may be comparatively cheaper but getting beyond the earth's atmosphere is the major problem.

For all its problems, however, space travel is the beacon that beckons yet.

A nightmare of ashes

In the film *Ground Zero Man* (1989) the hero says: 'In the '50s we thought of the atomic age as being as exciting as the space age was later'. This is in the context of a group of soldiers being exposed by their military superiors to radiation when placed too close to the 'ground zero' in an experimental test.

This is an image that dominates us now – and it is not a romantic one. Our vision of the atomic age is not positive. In Isaac Asimov's vignette, 'Hell-Fire' (1957), a slow-motion replay of a nuclear blast identifies the features of Satan on the developing mushroom cloud.[5]

We have repeatedly seen images of lunar rovers and space shuttles – but also ones of imitation human bodies being instantly fried as the nuclear blast hits them, of buildings disintegrating, of trees, landscapes being stripped bare. The initial bombs on Hiroshima and Nagasaki in 1945 were bad enough; and we all know about the enormously greater destruction now available to their successors. We have not been fooled by the process of disinformation and censorship that has sought to hide the unpalatable truth, the warnings about brown paper bags, mattresses, buckets of water and the like (as in Raymond Briggs' bitterly painful cartoon, 'When the Wind Blows', 1982). The banning of a film like Peter Watkins' *The War Game* in 1965 did not help: originally commissioned by the BBC, they were horrified at its accurately envisaged Armageddon, presented documentary-like.

Eventually other movies showed the same theme. In the USA, the terrifying films *The Day After* (1983) and *Terminator II: Judgement Day* (1991) respectively showed Laurence, Kansas and Los Angeles being blown apart in apocalyptic visions to haunt our nightmares. Even the BBC repented and showed one Sunday night in 1984 another work they had commissioned: *Threads* gave a bleak prospect of future war. The image of the mushroom cloud rising over the streets and houses of Sheffield is unforgettable. And, if one did survive the immediate onslaught, what of the aftermath – the disease, the plagues of rats and other vermin, the starvation, everybody's hand turned against everyone else, perhaps dying slowly and horribly and without painkillers from radiation poisoning? It would be better to be 'right underneath when the bomb dropped and pissed out of one's mind', understandably suggested someone when interviewed on TV the night after *Threads* was shown.

That same night a group of so-called experts and politicians discussed the even more terrifying scenario of nuclear winter. According to this, a relatively 'small nuclear exchange' (just 100 megatons on either side) might throw so much soot and material into the atmosphere as to obscure the sun's light for years over the whole of the planet. The result would be an enormous drop in temperature and the probable extinction of the human race. At the end of his TV series, *Civilisation*, Sir Kenneth Clark spoke gloomily of the prospects for the human future, one dominated by: 'the memory of that Shadowy Companion who is always with us, like an inverted Guardian Angel, silent, invisible, almost incredible, and yet unquestionably there'. Journalist John Tusa has said that the making of the atom bomb was like a second Fall, one that left humanity irrevocably changed.[6]

In other ways, too, the threat of nuclear holocaust has shown itself – the 1950s 'B' movies spoke of mutant creatures – spiders, ants, rats grown to huge size. In more recent decades we have grown morbidly suspicious of the supposedly good effects of atomic power. The (prophetic) film *The China Syndrome* (1979) was accompanied that year by the Three Mile Island disaster in New York State, while the Chernobyl episode affected people as far afield as Ireland. Meanwhile, the dream of 'safe' atomic fusion power seems as far away as ever. Used uranium remains lethally dangerous for thousands of years. Waste dealers struggle to find somewhere to accept their products.[7] The tiny South Pacific Island of Niue – like Western Samoa, Tonga and Fiji – has rejected millions of dollars in desperately needed revenue, offered in exchange for importing and incinerating tons of toxic waste. Even for countries as poor as these, it is just not worth it.

Could the scientists making the first atom bomb which was exploded at White Sands before being dropped on Hiroshima be totally sure they were not starting a chain reaction that would consume the whole planet? They were not. Sf writers dealt apocalyptically with that idea.[8] Then there are the stories where humans are reduced to vicious competition in the race for post-nuclear holocaust survival. In Ward Moore's *Lot* (1953), one ruthless, well organized man, trying to evacuate his family from a nuclear-threatened Los Angeles, eventually abandons his wife and brattish son at a service station: they are not regarded by him as worthy of survival. He only keeps his daughter who has a clear understanding of the sacrifices that must be made in this new world. Like Lot's wife, his wife is turned metaphorically into a pillar of salt as she looks back to her old life, refusing to abandon what must be given up in the harsh world that is to come. In his even bleaker and more cynical successor, *Lot's Daughter* (1954), Ward Moore envisages the father and daughter's future life together. 'Survivalism' is now a major growth area in the United States, with devotees taking weekends off to go into the wilderness to improvise a life without all the technological aids we take for granted.[9]

Children's comics stories are frequently set in a post-holocaust world. *2000 AD* has inexorable and invulnerable dispensers of arbitrary justice ('Judge Dredd'), perpetual cybernetic warfare ('Rogue Trooper') and everywhere a grim struggle for individual survival. This is a terrifying vision of the future that is being fed to our children. It is hardly surprising, then, that *Star Trek*'s optimism is so popular. Yet which do children believe? Maybe both.

A choice of futures

The future offers the possible realization of both the dream of stardust and the nightmare of atomic ashes; they are both rooted in the possibilities of today. Science fiction lies in the tension between them, the space that is created by time, by the 'not-yet'. Maybe we will blow ourselves up; maybe we will travel to other planets. Perhaps we will do both.

In Ray Bradbury's 1946 story, 'The Million-Year Picnic', the conclusion to his classic *Martian Chronicles*, a human colonist family travel out by boat to see the Martians, a race now fading towards extinction. After journeying a long way over the canals, the father tells his children to look down into the water. 'There they are' he says: they gaze at their own reflections. There are no native Martians left: they have been destroyed, deliberately and accidentally, by the human invaders. And now there are no humans left on earth either: they have destroyed themselves in nuclear war; no ships come from there any more. The shadow of Hiroshima lies heavily over this story, but more than that too – the effect of humans on others but also the hope of human transfiguration in space.

In this story Bradbury combines the two themes I have outlined: space travel and atomic warfare. Humanity, clever enough to escape its own planet, its place of birth, is stupid enough to have destroyed it as well. It is not necessarily a choice between the stars and nuclear holocaust. It may well be that we will get both at the same time. These are the science fiction alternatives which we shall discuss further in the pages that follow.

Chapter 2

The sense of wonder

What we get from science fiction . . . is not different from the thing that makes mainstream fiction rewarding, but only expressed differently. We live on a minute island of known things. Our undiminished wonder at the mystery which surrounds us is what makes us human. In science fiction we can approach that mystery, not in small, everyday symbols but in the big ones of space and time.

(Damon Knight) [1]

One of the classic definitions of science fiction is that it is based on the 'sense of wonder'. One of its early twentieth century progenitors, Jack Williamson, entitles his autobiography *Wonder's Child* (1984). Wonder stands at the beginning of the sf experience.

It has long been argued that wonder is a virtue. It is part of our gratitude for God's good creation that every day we should give thanks for what he has made. It does not simply mean being astonished at those things we see rarely (for example, Halley's Comet or the Aurora Borealis) but the ability to appreciate things that are there all the time – the love of our partner or family, the enjoyment of food or drink, all the 'humdrum' things of life we take for granted: all made by God and waiting to be enjoyed with gratitude. Some while ago I watched a programme on television which reminded me that caterpillars turn into butterflies. What an extraordinary thing! How had I forgotten it? Somehow it had become fossilized as a 'wonder of nature' in a schoolbook text on natural history, deprived of meaning or power.

In a similar way a great theologian has written of his own subject:

If anyone should not find himself astonished and filled with wonder when he becomes involved in one way or another with theology, he would be well advised to consider once more, from a certain remoteness and without prejudice, what is involved in this undertaking. The same holds true for anyone who should have accomplished the feat of no longer being astonished, instead of becoming continually more astonished all the time that he concerns himself with this subject.[2]

According to this view, wonder is at the heart of our apprehension of the world around us. It is our proper response to all that God has made for us, not to be taken for granted but with a due sense of thankfulness. In this sense, science fiction is fulfilling the divine imperative to expand our minds and hearts to appreciate all that he has made.

A seventeenth-century hymn expresses the same insight which is trumpeted a thousand times in science fiction:

> Now all the heavenly splendour
> Breaks forth in starlight tender
> From myriad worlds unknown;
> And man, the marvel seeing,
> Forgets his selfish being,
> For joy of beauty not his own.[3]

What is the relationship, then, between the science fiction notion of wonder and the Christian one, if indeed there is such a separate thing? The hymn makes its own connection:

> [Man's] care he drowneth yonder,
> lost in the abyss of wonder;
> to heaven his soul doth steal:
> this life he disesteemeth
> the day it is that dreameth,
> that doth from truth his vision seal.

What is central here is the idea of being caught up out of one's own immediate cares for the vision of something greater, overwhelming.

The 'other' and the 'different'

Science fiction, then, with its concentration on the extraordinary and unusual (impossible, often, within our present terms of reference) merely exaggerates what is a common element to all life. Science fiction speaks of this 'other' in terms of 'world-creation', the invention of a world that is different from this one in some significant respect. Such invention can either suggest a universe as strange as possible (with equally strange creatures inhabiting it), or one like ours – except for one vital difference. Bob Shaw provides a classic example in 'slow glass',[4] a material that accentuates the natural refractive qualities of actual glass so as to delay the transmission of images by years rather than microseconds. The ingenuity of the author is in developing the possible implications of such a development for human social life. Similarly, Isaac Asimov rings the changes with the idea of sentient robots, operating according to certain fixed laws, the 'Three Laws of Robotics'.

The notion that strangeness is the essence of science fiction is given further weight by the fact that the word 'alien' has become the password of science fiction. The delight of otherness (Latin *alienus* means 'other') – strangeness, the unknown – is both attractive and alarming, enticing and discomforting. One classic definition of the 'holy' is Rudolf Otto's 'numinous': *mysterium tremendum et fascinans* ('the terrifying and fascinating mystery').

There is in fact so much 'alienness' on this planet, everything that is different from what we are used to, what is unfamiliar, what is challenging in asking that we open ourselves up to the different, and become a learner again. This is something that science fiction offers us. In the words of *Star Trek*'s Captains Kirk and Picard, science fiction portrays strange new worlds, new life and new civilizations, places to explore, places 'to boldly go where no one has gone before'. It depicts a galaxy of stars through which mile-long spaceships roam, encountering aliens of peculiar colour, many arms and revolting habits. On strange planets anything can happen; life can manifest itself in a thousand disguises – from chameleon-like protoplasm to planetwide cells with a passion for extra-planetary expansion. It can be vegetable, crystalline, silicon, swarms of cybernetic machines, even a nanobyte-filled metallic river sabotaged by cyberterrorists from Greenpeace.[5] Even in more recognizable forms, it could vary from the the bear-like Kzinti and ostrichlike Pierson's Puppeteers of Larry Niven's *Tales of Known Space* (1966–7) to the same author's huge Bandersnatchi, hypnotic Grogs and rocket like Stage Trees. There could be a 25-mile deep hole on one planet or a world with time flowing at different rates on different latitudes on its surface on another.[6] Within the solar system sf imagined desiccated and jungle-ridden Venerian landscapes, sleeting Jovian storms and rose-red desert-hidden Martian cities[7] – visions which work their magic still, inaccurate as scientific probes may have shown them to be. The quest for life in improbable places produced planets like Hal Clements' 'Whirligig World' with hardy inhabitants who defy the problems of living on a world so flattened that its gravity varies from 3 G at the equator to a massive 700 G at the poles. Huge mountains might be shaped like women, an empire stretch over a galaxy.[8]

Science fiction offers up a multitude of novel possibilities for writers and readers who adored the unusual, the extreme, the bizarre, the *different*. What we are offered is a world conclusively different to the familiar one, even if what is presented can be argued as in George Orwell's *1984* (1949), or Aldous Huxley's *Brave New World* (1932) to be a plausible development of present tendencies, readily visible now to those with eyes to see. In so far as this is the case, science fiction claims to be prophetic literature, pointing out what is to happen before it happens. Alternatively, it can try to portray how things might have been otherwise, given a change in one small but critical historical nexus: a world in which the Confederates won the battle of Gettysburg, the Spanish Armada successfully invaded England, the Axis won the Second World War.[9] Such 'alternate' or 'parallel' universe stories can concentrate attention not only on the central change factors of history but also on the sheer extraordinariness of what actually is the case – and indeed even to give thanks for it. (Very few alternate future histories are benign: in *Dr Who* and *Star Trek* timetravel stories the future of the

Earth or even the universe is usually at stake.) As much as any branch of science fiction, this subgenre highlights science fiction's sheer love of play, of speculation.

Science fiction – a brief history

Much has been written of the origins of science fiction, and some writers are fond of finding its hoary antecedents dating back as far as Homer's *Odyssey* and Lucian of Samosata's *True History*. There is perhaps more of a case for seeing a connection with works dating from the beginning of what we might call the modern period. Such works might include the *Utopia* of Thomas More (1516), the *New Atlantis* of Francis Bacon (1626) and the travelling fantasies of Johannes Kepler (1634) and Cyrano de Bergerac (1657). As well as imaginary voyages to the moon, journeys to the centre of the earth, as in works by Ludvig Holberg (1741), were proposed.

To some extent, these speculations can be seen as a natural correlate to the age of discovery. It was not till the end of the nineteenth century, when the vast unmapped spaces on earth had been conclusively filled, that speculation about unknown places and people needed to be transferred beyond the earth's atmosphere.

Towards the turn of the eighteenth century, the scientific revolution began to make itself felt in people's lives at all levels. The age of the cities was upon us, and primarily upon Britain, which at this time led the way in applying technology. The first steam locomotive was produced in 1829 by George Stephenson. Simultaneously, people were beginning to think differently about the world. Charles Darwin's grandfather, Erasmus Darwin, had formulated in his *Zoonomia* (1794, 1796) a picture of a world of infinitely greater age than had been previously thought. Categories such as that of evolution began to make themselves present to the mental map of industrial humanity. Change became noticeable in people's lifetimes and was accompanied by its ideology.[10] Not only was change happening (went this theory) but it was a good thing. Unemployed Luddite workers who attacked the machinery that had replaced them were wrong because they stood 'in the way of progress'. The 'myth of progress', the most significant scientific worldview of our time, is an amalgamation of the idea of technological progress with a Darwinian view of biological evolution.

It was at this time that Mary Wollstonecraft Shelley drafted *Frankenstein or The Modern Prometheus*, the novel now accepted by many as the first real science fiction story. The cultural possibility of scientific, rational, technological humanity contemplating both fearfully and excitedly its future began to arise in earnest. Above all, there was the hope of a humanity freed from the vices and traditions of the past, free to seek its own destiny.

In America, Edgar Allan Poe wrote horror fiction in a vein that touched on the new scientific possibilities, whilst in France Jules Verne loudly celebrated the virtues of the new technology. H. G. Wells wrote a whole series of complex and satisfying novels towards the turn of the nineteenth century, laying down much of the groundwork for future discussion.

The English writer Brian Stableford has argued that at this point science fiction takes a sharp split between its British and American forms. In Britain the tradition of Shelley and Wells was continued in the form of the 'Scientific Romance'. This genre remained part of the literary mainstream, one in which writers such as C. S. Lewis, George Orwell, Aldous Huxley, Angus Wilson and Kingsley Amis (among others) could indulge without fear of ridicule. In the United States the story was rather different.

America had by now surpassed Britain, and indeed everyone else, at the forefront of technological change. Thomas Edison's inventions of the telephone and light bulb were creating the basis for the life most of us take for granted; Henry Ford with his Model T car was initiating a new era of mass transportation. In the painting of early American modernism, the machine became a deeply romanticized cult object. New York above all was portrayed as the city of the future, 'the Gothic arches of a bridge like a cathedral to progress, symbolising engineering as myth'.[11]

The science fiction that arose in the USA was along the same lines. Hugo Gernsback's first pulp sf magazine, *Amazing Stories* (1926) represented a kind of technological Masonic movement, effectively serving to 'ghettoize' sf. Gernsback's

own novel *Ralph 124C41 +* (1925) has minimal characterization and is barely literate, but reveals an extraordinary belief
in the utopian powers of science and technology. As well as
frequent breathless naivety, pulp writing was full of colour,
adventure and freshness. The Frank R. Paul covers of *Amazing
Stories*, *Air Wonder Stories* and *Science Wonder Stories* embody
this age: vast interplanetary ships crusing through space,
huge futuristic cities. Typical writers of this period are Jack
Williamson, Edmond Hamilton, John Campbell Jnr, Stanley
Weinbaum and E. E. 'Doc' Smith. 'Space opera' (romantic
tales of interstellar conflict) was the norm.

When John Campbell became editor of *Astounding Stories*
in 1939 he changed its title to *Astounding Science Fiction*
(*ASF*). For many, it represented the so-called 'Golden Age' of
science fiction, lasting under Campbell's guidance till the
late 1960s. Many speak of the 'power fantasies' advocated
and supported by Campbell. Whatever one's opinions of his
right-wing, social Darwinian political views and idiosyncratic
enthusiasms for pseudo-science (psionic machines, the Dean
Drive, the proto-Scientology Dianetics of L. Ron Hubbard
and the like), there is no doubt that he revolutionized pulp
sf. Under his guidance, a new generation of science fiction
writers developed – Robert Heinlein, Isaac Asimov, Clifford
Simak and Theodore Sturgeon among others. By 1950
Campbell had moved away from gee-whiz astonishment at
technology to a deliberate policy of investigation of its social
and political consequences. In the many new magazines
which emerged at that time (*Galaxy* and *The Magazine of
Fantasy and Science Fiction* in particular) there was a concentration on sociology, often of a satirical bent, from writers
such as Frederick Pohl and C. M. Kornbluth, and a greater
emphasis on style. Whilst to many this was long overdue, it
was seen by others as a retrogression to the common standards of the mainstream. Whilst still driven by demands of
its clientele and editors, science fiction began to expand in
different directions, attracting new authors such as James
Blish, Poul Anderson and Walter M. Miller Jnr.

This was also the age of the 1950s 'B' movies. Cheaply
made, without major stars and with rather basic special
effects, these nevertheless attracted sympathetic audiences,

drawn by their topicality. They explored, often in metaphor, possibilities of global cataclysm and societal takeover, whilst suggesting new perspectives on humanity's relation to the universe. With titles like *The Day the Earth Stood Still* (1951), *This Island Earth* (1955), *Destination Moon* (1950) and *Invasion of the Body Snatchers* (1956), they drew a new audience to science fiction. In a similar way, sf was also to be found on radio and TV: in the UK Charles Chilton's *Journey into Space* enthralled radio listeners in the early 1950s as did Angus MacVicar's *Lost Planet* stories and then *Quatermass* on TV. These paved the way for *Dr Who* (from 1963) with its cardboard sets and plastic monsters watched in trepidation from behind the sofa, as did series such as *The Twilight Zone* (1959–64) in the USA for the equally longlived *Star Trek* (from 1966). Such programmes and stories were often primitive, with corny characters, stereotyped plots and dubious science at best – but they had a freshness, innocence and energy that so much today has lost. As J. G. Ballard has observed, NASA did a grave disservice to space travel in making it so deliberately prosaic.[12] Then, however, everything was new and exciting. Sputnik had just been launched: the space race had arrived.

One new author of the 1960s was Frank Herbert (notably with his cult success, *Dune*), whilst others already writing such as Brian Aldiss and Philip K. Dick came to greater prominence. Throughout the whole of this period, Arthur C. Clarke, the founder of the British Interplanetary Society, continued to pour out a series of elegiac stories in support of technology.

In the middle of the 1960s, a crisis hit science fiction on both sides of the Atlantic. This is often given the name of 'the New Wave', and was characterized by rebelliousness, stylistic experiment and discussion of hitherto-forbidden themes such as sexuality, violence and religion (notably in Harlan Ellison's 1967 ground-breaking anthology, *Dangerous Visions*): a content, above all, where the hero's destination was more likely to be bed than Mars. In Britain, this movement was headed by the Arts Council-sponsored *New Worlds* magazine under the editorship of Michael Moorcock, who proceeded to develop a new generation of writers such as J. G. Ballard. It is said that for many sf writers Ballard's stories 'are simply unforgiveable. They take the upwardly mobile imagery of sf and transform it into a litany of loss, decline and death.' Thomas M. Disch too was unpopular with readers for his pessimism regarding humanity: of his novel *334* (1972), it has been said that there is no hero and no hope.[13] Whilst Disch's attitude was innovative for an American writer, it followed George Orwell's celebrated vision of the future, 'a boot stamping on the human face forever', a conclusion which, whether 'plausible or not, . . . almost no orthodox science-fiction writer would admit'.[14]

The impact of the New Wave is uncertain. Some writers, such as Isaac Asimov, declared themselves frightened by it. It is arguable how far or how radically it affected the genre. Some, like Samuel Delany and Roger Zelazny at the end of the 1960s grew under its influence, whilst others such as the prolific Robert Silverberg continued to pour out works in their usual vein. The imaginative Ursula K. Le Guin was a new star, whilst Larry Niven was a popular and competent exponent of so-called 'hard sf', science fiction using established or carefully-extrapolated science as its backbone.

In the 1970s Joe Haldeman's *The Forever War* (1974) enshrined the author's cynical experiences of Vietnam whilst Joanna Russ represented in some ways the forefront of a new wave of feminist sf. Notable writers of the 1980s and 1990s have included cyberpunk pioneer William Gibson, Greg Bear, David Brin, Iain M. Banks, Paul McAuley and Dan Simmons. There have also been an increasing number of women writers such as Gwyneth Jones, Lois McMaster Bujold, C. J. Cherryh and Pat Cadigan. Sheri S. Tepper, Margaret Attwood, Marion Zimmer Bradley, Marge Piercy and 'James Tiptree Jnr' (Alice Sheldon) have utilized sf's ability to envisage alternate societies to (often savagely) critique what they regarded as the injustices of a patriarchal society. This enablement of conscious expressions of discontent at the status quo follows a tradition that goes back at least as far as the satire of Swift's *Gulliver's Travels* (1726). A field of articulate feminist sf criticism has arisen, analysing both the male assumptions of the genre and dreaming of a world in which women do not exist only, as one title put it,

In the Chinks of the World Machine (1988). In that book, Sarah Lefanu argued that sf allows women to speak in their own voices, freed from the imprisoning conventionalities of 'normal' fiction.

Meanwhile, the films of the late 1970s rediscovered the 'space opera' of the 1930s and with it some (albeit nostalgic) energy. *Star Wars* (1977, together with its sequels) derived from director George Lucas' love for the *Buck Rogers* serials of his youth, but with modern day special effects. Science fiction was uncertain how to come to terms with its own success: Brian Aldiss described *Star Wars* as 'an outsize elephant with the brains of a gnat . . . . All we had once hoped for came true. Wishes were granted – always a perilous process.'[15] We beheld desert, ice, swamp and forest worlds, whirling asteroids and cities in the clouds – and were convinced. In *The Quiet Earth* (1985), a man stands alone on a beach, dwarfed by an enormous ringed planet rising behind him; in *Waterworld* (1995) an island is surrounded by oceans stretching around the rest of the Earth. The image is all, suggestive of changed reality, 'more a state of ecstasy than a sense of wonder'.[16] Steven Spielberg's movies (*Close Encounters of the Third Kind*, 1977; *E.T.*, 1982) were rhapsodic along the lines of the 'cool romanticism' of Stanley Kubrick's classically realistic but deeply emotional *2001: A Space Odyssey* (1968). By contrast, Ridley Scott's *Alien* (1979) and *Blade Runner* (1982) painted the downside of life in the future.

So where are we now in the written form of the genre? Some sf writers like Frederick Pohl seem to go on forever. Although Heinlein and Asimov have now died, their work remains popular. The most recent work by them and Arthur C. Clarke has been notable for its length. Rather than the short stories of the 1940s and 1950s, later developed or 'fixed up' into novels, new science fiction works have tended to be inordinately long, with a vast array of characters interweaving in complicated manner. Here they have become like the fantasy works with which they so often appear side by side on library and airport bookshelves, and which have also shown an extraordinary growth in popularity. Though, in the latter case, this was largely precipitated by the success of J. R. R. Tolkien's *The Lord of the Rings* (1954–55), most fantasy has long since abandoning that work's Christian substratum and subtleties. This is seen both in films, in which a simple-minded portrayal of extreme good and evil is repeated ad nauseam, and in books. In science fiction, by contrast, there there is often complexity as well as invention, a subtlety that may blur into obscurity. It is worth comparing these two related, but different, genres in some detail.

Science fiction and fantasy

It has been said that science fiction deals with improbable possibilities, fantasy with plausible impossibilities.[17] Although both sf and fantasy are based on wonder, sf claims, at least in theory, to dwell in the realm of the feasible. Here it differs from fantasy, which also delights in other worlds of the imagination, but patently unreal ones – worlds inhabited by elves, dwarves and trolls. For all this, magazines as trenchantly committed to technophiliac science fiction as *Science Fiction Age* include fantasy stories without embarrassment and with scarcely a murmur of protest from their readers. Both genres, indeed, pose of alternatives to our present world and challenge our normal understanding of reality. What they share is greater than what separates them.

We may develop the definition of sf as comprehending both science and technology. Sf's view of humanity as both *homo cognoscens* ('knowing humanity') and *homo faber* ('humanity the maker') leads to Tom Shippey's definition of it as 'fabril literature'.[18] According to this view, the crucial image of science fiction is seen in Stanley Kubrick's film, *2001: A Space Odyssey*. An apeman, in a burst of intelligence, uses a bone to kill a rival. In triumph he hurls it into the air where, rotating – and to the whirling strains of a Strauss waltz – it is transformed into an orbiting space station. This vast cosmic conceit has a clear message: humanity is consti-tuted by its tools. The opposable thumb which gives humanity a better grasp of weapons sets it 'on the path to the stars'.[19] And, in this model, violence is a part of the way forward. It symbolizes humanity's control over its environ-ment – if not over itself.

'Fabril' literature is the opposite of 'pastoral' literature, says

Shippey. 'Pastoral literature is rural, nostalgic, conservative. It idealises the past and tends to convert complexities into simplicities; the central image lies in the shepherd. Fabril literature . . . is overwhelmingly urban, disruptive, future-oriented, eager for novelty; its central image is the "faber", the smith or blacksmith in older usage, but now extended in science fiction to mean the creator of artefacts in general – metallic, crystalline, genetic, or even social.' It is thus concerned with humanity's impact on its environment; 'at the same time it is more and more aware of the immense scale of Nature, against which human beings are set and against which they are ultimately powerless'.[20] In works like Mary Shelley's *The Last Man* (1826), H. G. Wells' *The Time Machine* (1895) and Michael Crichton's *Jurassic Park* (1990), we see humanity's courage, ingenuity and technology come to naught against the forces of nature. This encounter between humanity and nature is of the essence of sf.

In this science fiction world, it is generally the scientists (as in Fred Hoyle's *The Black Cloud*, 1957, or the multitudinous stories of *Dr Who*) who are right. Others may be over-belligerent or, alternatively, naively unwary (*Independence Day*); only those who 'know' can be trusted. Indeed in Larry Niven and Jerry Pournelle's epic *Footfall* (1985), it is science fiction writers themselves who are the sages in a situation that they alone have anticipated – alien invasion.

Sf takes people out of the land and asks what is their relation to it; in fantasy, by contrast, they are at home in it. Fantasy is 'pastoral', static and conservative, sf 'fabril', dynamic and radical. In the works of J. R. R. Tolkien, the forces of 'progress' are identified with the smoking engines, turning wheels and felled trees of the evil Sauron and Saruman. For him, technology is the enemy or, at least, the tool of the enemy. Yet fantasy too in its own way is concerned with human power, with the ability to act as well as be: 'sword and sorcery' is its equivalent to spaceships and computers. Magic is its knowledge and control, tuned to the powers of the world in its own way. Here, it may be argued, science fiction and fantasy come together. Indeed, Arthur C. Clarke's 'Third Law' declares that 'any sufficiently advanced technology is indistinguishable from magic'.[21]

If our culture is full of sf, what does this say of the genre's future? Does it speak to us of the future or the present? Culturally, Mr Spock and Luke Skywalker are as much a part of our contemporary scene as the Arthurian Knights were of Shakespearian England's. Films such as Robert Zemeckis' *Back To The Future* (1985) have made us all blithely competent at handling typical science fiction ideas such as time paradoxes. It is not merely a matter of imagination, however; if we know the jargon, we also daily experience the reality. We live in a science fiction world.

Chapter 3

The crucible of science fiction

It was on a dreary night of November, that I beheld the accomplishment of my toils. With an anxiety that almost amounted to agony, I collected the instruments of life around me, that I might infuse a spark of being into the lifeless thing that lay at my feet. It was already one in the morning; the rain pattered dismally against the panes, and my candle was nearly burnt out, when, by the glimmer of the half-extinguished light, I saw the dull yellow eye of the creature open; it breathed hard, and a convulsive motion agitated its limbs.

(Mary Shelley, *Frankenstein*)[1]

Thus was born Frankenstein's monster and, with it, sf. Much has been written of the parentage of sf. H. G. Wells (treated later in this chapter), Jules Verne, Hugo Gernsback and John W. Campbell have all been credited with its paternity. Recent opinion, however, concurs that its mother was Mary Wollstonecraft Shelley (1797–1851) and, in the light of her work, doubts indeed whether any father as such is needed.

Mary Shelley

The parents themselves of the author of *Frankenstein or The Modern Prometheus* were intellectual innovators. Mary's mother was Mary Wollstonecraft, a noted feminist and educationalist, the author of *A Vindication of the Rights of Women* (1792), who died giving birth to her; her father was William Godwin, a rationalist philosopher and novelist. Mary herself eloped with the poet Percy Bysshe Shelley (who had been expelled from Oxford University for atheism) and fled to the

26

Continent where two years later, and after his first wife had committed suicide, they married. In more than one way, therefore, she stands at the gate of the modern age.

She wrote *Frankenstein* at a famous literary party on the shores of Lake Geneva in 1816 that included her husband, the scandalous Lord Byron and Dr John Polidori. Locked in by the rain and impressed by some German ghost stories, Byron proposed that they should write ones of their own: Mary's was the result of listening to Byron and Shelley's speculations on new scientific possibilities, animated in the crucible of her nightly imagination: the vision with which this chapter began. Only Mary's and Polidori's stories came to anything (that latter was published as *The Vampyre* in 1819). *Frankenstein* – published in 1818 – has become as famous as anything that her notorious companions – then the toasts of Europe – ever published. According to Brian Aldiss, 'the elements of that novel are still being explored in fiction, because they are still of seminal interest to our technological society'.[2]

It is often thought that science fiction's roots are rationalistic – the battle of science against superstition. This is only partially true: there is also a strong Romantic element to the beginning of sf. Romanticism reacted against the cool rationalism of the Enlightenment, expressing itself in the passionate self-expression of people like Goethe, Beethoven and the English Romantic poets. It was the time of the German artistic movement *Sturm und Drang* ('Storm and Stress'), of the American and French Revolutions, of the threat of change everywhere. Whilst seemingly at odds with rationalism, Romanticism shared with it a crucial emphasis on the human being as subject. As we shall see, this is central to sf. Gothic literature was the particular form in which Romanticism chiefly moulded science fiction. The word itself derives from architecture and declares a nostalgic and utterly unrealistic desire to return to the Middle Ages. Gothic emphasized dread and horror, weirdness and strangeness. Horace Walpole's *The Castle of Otranto* (1765), subtitled 'A Gothic Story', set a trend; it is estimated that as many as five thousand similar works followed. (Jane Austen's *Northanger Abbey* is a spoof.) Science fiction values Gothic emotions, says Aldiss, but transfers them from lonely castles, ghosts, blood, cliffs and wild seas to alien spacecraft, planets, tentacular beings and incomprehensible paranormal powers. Classic Gothic themes are constraint, threatened identity, pursuit, arcane experimentation, evil.[3] *The X-Files* (1993–) has strong Gothic elements.

The Preface to *Frankenstein* begins by referring to Erasmus Darwin, Charles Darwin's grandfather and 'some of the physiological writers of Germany'. It is claimed that these give scientific underpinning to the tale that follows. This is the fundamental claim of sf, that – unlike fantasy – its speculations are grounded on real science, how the world actually is. Thus, for example, when *Jurassic Park* came out, much was made of the scientific possibilities of restoring dinosaur DNA from insects trapped in amber millions of year old. Sf's appeal is to the authority of science, to inherit its mantle and thus to claim to be talking about reality.

In the story Baron Frankenstein leaves his home for the University of Ingolstadt; there, however, he turns in disgust from his studies, deciding that 'the learning he had acquired from ancient books is false and that modern science offers truer and more efficacious insights'.[4] Shelley's basis for Frankenstein's invention is the new science of Galvanism. Rather as electrical currents cause the limbs of dead frogs to jerk, Frankenstein will literally shock the monster into existence with the 'spark of life'.

There is in this a deliberate turning one's back on the past and seeking instead a future created by science. In so doing, Frankenstein crosses old boundaries, daring to create life itself. Like Marlowe's Dr Faustus, he exclaims, 'so much has been done . . . more, far more, will I achieve'. Aldiss adds: 'the Faustian theme is brought dramatically up to date, with science replacing supernatural machinery'.[5] Nothing will be beyond humanity's grasp when it is liberated from the dead weight and moral prejudices of the past.

The creation, however, does not go well: Frankenstein recoils in horror from what he has made. The monster, originally innocent, is corrupted by its maker's rejection and then that of others. What was intended as a new Adam increasingly is called a 'fiend', 'the fallen angel' becomes 'a malignant devil'. It demands a mate and, when this is refused, murders its creator's wife and brother in revenge. Frankenstein sets out to track it down, a pursuit that eventually ends in the arctic wastes. Frankenstein is killed; his creature disappears across the ice floes.

The act of creation is an act of blasphemy that crosses moral frontiers. It encroaches on God's traditional prerogatives. Shelley quotes from Milton's *Paradise Lost* (X. 743–5) to indicate the creature's ambivalent reaction to being created:

> Did I request thee, Maker, from my clay
> To mould me man? Did I solicit thee
> From darkness to promote me?

Sf arrives, says Brian Aldiss, in the heart and crucible of the English Romantic movement with 'a discreetly blasphemous nature that it still retains'. It is no coincidence that this is a time when 'Western man began to alter his attitude towards his God . . . . The concept of Frankenstein rests on the quasi-evolutionary idea that God is remote or absent from creation: man therefore is free to create his own sub-life.'[6] Aldiss would have us remember Shelley's atheism.

Inherent in the story, then, is the idea of humanity 'playing' God or, rather, 'replacing' God. That the result is disastrous is seminal for sf: as Aldiss says, 'inside Mary Shelley's novel lie the seeds of all later diseased creation myths, including H. G. Wells' *Island of Dr Moreau*, and the legions of robots from Capek's[7] day forward'. In the light of Hiroshima, 1950s Hollywood 'B' movies repeated the theme that there are 'some things that we are not meant to know' (or to do).[8] In the 1980s the eco-thriller *Edge of Darkness* hinted at the revenge of a nature that is fed up with being 'meddled with', and in the 1990s so did the fictional dinosaurs of *Jurassic Park*. Meanwhile the very real cows suffering from the dreadful disease of BSE offered the Prince of Wales the opportunity to suggest that '*Frankenstein*-like' manipulation of nature has crossed into 'realms that belong to God, and to God alone'.[9] Whether this is true or not is irrelevant to the fact that it is God's absence which is essential for the context both of *Frankenstein* and sf.

This idea of limits is central to sf: are there any? If so, who decides them and what will be the consequences if we break them? Frankenstein consistently breaks all the old ones. He is ruthless in pursuit of his aims and even allows an innocent woman to be executed for a crime committed by the monster in order to protect it. The notion that his scientific work is too important to be imperilled by any traditional moral consideration is typical of the scary utilitarian messianism we find in some later science fiction; it rings of Hitler and Stalin's sacrifice of millions of people in pursuit of a supposedly transcendent goal. It is savagely caricatured by C. S. Lewis in his picture of Weston and N.I.C.E. in his space trilogy.

Frankenstein is not Mary Shelley's only work. *The Last Man* (1826), whilst by no means so well known, deals with an equally significant science fiction theme: human extinction at the hands of natural disaster. In various forms that too has laid the groundwork for the future. It anticipates the whole 'disaster', 'cataclysms and dooms', 'holocaust and catastrophe' brand of science fiction. It faces up to the problem of humanity's future − when there is no God to bring an end to things. It is secular eschatology.

What is pivotal to sf is not just the supposed blasphemy of Frankenstein. It is the fundamental ambiguity of that act. Frankenstein's creation of life is a monumental, towering achievement, one to be honoured and admired. Yet it is also flawed by reason of its creator − that is, humanity's − own troubled nature. Science fiction stands in this place of ambiguity. It oscillates between optimism and pessimism, utopia and dystopia, pride and despair. Humanity can reach the stars or it can destroy itself in nuclear war. Stardust *or* ashes, one might say. Brian Aldiss is not unaware of this: in his own novel, *Frankenstein Unbound* (1973), which he wrote simultaneously with his history of sf, a future humanity does not inaugurate the vaunted Earthly Paradise but rather annihilates itself through its own hubristic meddling.

Theologians have summarized humanity's condition without God in exactly this way. Karl Barth wrote that 'the swing to and fro between pride and anxiety is human life'.[10] Jürgen Moltmann argues that the twin sins of pride and despair contradict the true nature of hope.[11] Despair is the disillusioned opposite pole of pride. Pride is when we think we can make it; despair is when we find out we cannot.

In this very ambiguity, humanity's relation to the universe that surrounds it takes on enormous importance. Without the 'great Other' of God, the lesser others of created existence become more significant, helping to define who we are. These may be other beings, sentient or otherwise (aliens); they may be creatures of our own making (monsters or machines); they may be the other into which we develop (superhumans).[12] Alternatively, they may be impersonal 'Nature' itself. This was a period of the discovery of Nature as well as of humanity as an acting subject. The two interconnected in the new recreation of mountain-climbing, something incomprehensible in an earlier time when mountains were just a nuisance! We should not forget the geographical location of *Frankenstein*'s writing – which is also the setting of the novel. Lake Geneva is moody, sunny one moment, stormy the next, surrounded by the towering Alps, part of the wider world that English people were beginning to discover as they undertook the 'Grand Tour'. The Antarctic wastes that surround the final battle of Frankenstein and his creature are not accidental either. A painting of the period, shows a crushed ship dwarfed by surrounding ice-floes: its title is 'The Wreck of the *Hope*'. As has been written: 'Romanticism arose from "a single I" opposed to an immense "not-I". This situation stimulated powerful self-awareness and proud subjectivism, but also a sense of bewilderment and abandon.'[13] This questioning of the relation of humanity to the wider cosmos is of the essence of sf. Sf's emphasis on size, the big time, the fate of species, worlds and universes, is a direct inheritance from Romanticism.

Our age has replaced eternity with a worship of time and matter. Change is not merely alteration: it is development, growth, progress. This is the result of combining 'immanentism' – the significance of the here and now – with idealism. The result is a kind of spirituality of materialism. For all its rejection of religion, science fiction invests the universe with depths of transcendence.

Similarly, the constancy of the person has been dissolved into the momentariness of the act. What you do is more

important than who you are: it is all you are. Triviality follows
because the wellsprings of human conduct are poorly understood. Amelioration is seen in terms of changing people's
actions – rather than changing the person who performs
those actions. This failure to comprehend the fundamental
roots of problems leads to a superficiality in our contemporary
world, and correspondingly in science fiction as one of its
expressions.

One further note that can be made is to observe the way
in which most people associate *Frankenstein* with horror
rather than science fiction (courtesy of Boris Karloff); in a
similar way, the name 'Frankenstein' has become associated
with the monster rather than his creator. Rather than being
a deviation from the significance of the work, it could be
argued to highlight it. Horror expresses the anxiety that
science does not explain everything after all, that rationalism
is not the whole answer, that there are 'more things in heaven
and earth . . . than are dreamt of in your philosophy' (*Hamlet*,
I. 5). In other words, the Enlightenment notion of a coolly
rational, autonomous humanity is far from the truth. Goya's
painting: 'The Dream of Reason Produces Monsters'[14]
exemplifies this fear. Modern horror fiction in the manner of
James Herbert or Stephen King continues this sceptical
reaction to Enlightenment rationalism. Horror is almost
always concerned with lack of freedom. Werewolves and
vampires are doomed to their fate; with sickening inevitability the protagonists of horror films go blindly to their doom.
It is fate, not freedom, that is predominant. In this way,
horror is part of our disillusionment with modernism, the
belief that through our 'knowledge' and 'control' of the world
we have unprecedented ability to control our own destiny.
The number of 'Mysteries of the Unknown' type programmes
on TV witnesses to this collapse in trust in rationalistic
modernism, as much as it does to our credulity.

The fear expressed in modern horror derives not from
known dangers but from unknown, implausible ones. AIDS,
terrorist bombs, cancer, traffic accidents, nuclear contamina-
tion, plane crashes, wars, sexual assaults, pornography, famine,
plague, floods are obviously not enough! We have to worry
about gremlins behind the TV set, malign occultic powers,

pyroclastic teenagers, werewolves and Satan-worshipping Nazis. One could argue that this supposedly rationalist, modern society is one of the most credulous and superstitious ever in history. Belief in astrology, flying saucers, crop circles, pyramids, copper bracelets, pyramids, crystals, the Bermuda Triangle and so forth is rampant. Or, in the words of the aphorism popularly attributed to G. K. Chesterton, 'when people cease to believe in God, they don't believe in nothing; they believe in anything'. Does not horror fiction reveal that modern godless society stands anxiously trembling on the brink of the unknown?

The conceptual abandonment of God

How did the belief in the absence of God come about? The conventional view is of the growth and success of science which made belief in God firstly unnecessary and then untenable. As has been said, however, the myths of the warfare of science and religion are almost always untrue – and this one is too. The conceptual abandonment of God was the result of a long development in the history of thought.

As the Middle Ages drew to a close about the year 1500, a number of subtle and widespread changes were taking place. Alongside the Renaissance and Reformation came the growth of science in its modern form. During the scientific revolution of the sixteenth and seventeenth centuries both scientific knowledge and method accelerated drastically. Medieval European science had depended much for its basic structure on the knowledge of the ancient Greeks, transmitted via the Arabs especially in the twelfth century and from the influx of Byzantine refugees fleeing the fall of Constantinople to the Turks in 1453.

Significant as this was, however, many have argued that the conceptual foundations of science were laid during the Middle Ages by the Judaeo-Christian belief in one God who creates a free, contingent universe. This belief in a 'universe' – rather than a pluriverse[15] – is one of the bases of modern science, along with correlate beliefs in its coherence, intelligibility and consistency. All these things science (popularly supposed to be based only on proof) takes for granted as unquestioned axioms, and it could not operate if it did not. However, all these things also hang on the universe's contingency, that is, the fact that things could be otherwise. What this means is that the truth about the universe is to be discovered by examining and testing it, not by armchair speculation and abstract reasoning from supposedly self-evident principles. In a necessary universe, the latter method would work; in a contingent one, the seeker after knowledge has to get his hands dirty. This is the basis of the 'scientific method', the way of experiment.

This may seem obvious to us, yet it was far from so to the Ancients and Medievals. Neoplatonic and Pythagorean thinking tended to discourage scientific investigation by asserting that science was deducible from logical first principles, that is, purely conceptually as necessary laws. It was, for example, assumed that, since the heavens were self-evidently divine, motion there would be in the perfect form of the circle. It was not till Kepler was forced reluctantly to investigate whether planetary motions were better explained by the ellipse that this particular idea was questioned. As a number of theoreticians like Thomas Kuhn have shown, such systems as the third-century Ptolemaic 'paradigm' are remarkably resistant to changes. The medieval system was a highly elevated one: it was thought that through meditation on earthly, temporal realities, one could rise to contemplation of heavenly, eternal ones. The Augustinian sacramental universe gave a largely referential value to this world. Medieval bestiaries depicted animals as symbolizing eternal, intellectual virtues: the deer swiftness (of thought as well as of body), the snake subtlety, the lamb innocence, the eagle wisdom and so forth. Inherent in Christianity was a belief in the value of the creaturely world, one made and redeemed by God, but this insight had to fight against the inherited weight of traditional views supported by the giants of the past. If Aristotle asserted that the world was eternal, or rest was the natural state of objects and all motion had to be separately explained, it was hard to disagree.[16]

By contrast, the scientific revolution was part of a movement of thought that took the world seriously in its own right, and said that it should dictate how to understand it. Till this happened, science could never properly take off. Alexander Pope's *Essay on Man* (1733–4), sums up the enterprise:

> Know then thyself, presume not God to scan,
> The proper study of Mankind is Man.

In other words, in order to understand the world, one did not look at God, but at the world. By parallel, in order to understand God one does not look at the world but at God and lets him declare himself in sovereign freedom in revelation. This rediscovery of God's Word in the Reformation was accompanied by the scientific affirmation of letting the world disclose itself without presuppositions. For this reason, some have identified the Reformation as being of pivotal significance to the next stage in the development of thought. Autonomy was given to science to develop in its own way, *etsi deus non daretur*, 'as if God were not given'. To know the world did not require knowing its Creator. The earliest scientists (people like Bacon, Copernicus, Newton, even Galileo) were not atheists but devout Christians, but the relevant point is that they did not have to be.

As time went on science developed its own momentum. The scientific method, the way of experiment, was postulated by Francis Bacon who said that one 'tormented nature' to get its secrets from it. The world increasingly was seen as a mechanism that operated according to a 'closed continuum of cause and effect', that is, completely internally, without any requirement for anything outside the system. This is famously summed up by the story of the visit of the Emperor Napoleon to the astronomer Laplace at the beginning of the nineteenth century; after Laplace had explained the movements of the heavenly spheres, Napoleon asked about God's place in all the complex workings. To this Laplace simply replied, 'I have no need of that hypothesis!'. This is the deathknell of the 'God of the gaps'. This is a redundant God who has been squeezed beyond the world, the God of Stephen Hawking and Carl Sagan. Sagan writes in the former's *A Brief History of Time* that there is no need for God 'for there is nothing for a Creator to do'.[17]

In such a self-explanatory world, it becomes difficult to justify miracles or prayer or indeed any kind of activity by

God at all. If there is a God, he must be remote. Maybe he 'kick-started' the whole thing off, like the watchmaker of William Paley's famous argument, but he is no longer relevant, no longer involved. During the nineteenth and twentieth centuries we have become used to the claim that the things science talks about are the only ones worth talking about, and – by extension – the only things one can talk about. This is the omniscient attitude of both logical positivism and of modern scientistic popularizers like Peter Atkins.[18]

The science which was built on Christianity required conceptual independence from it in order to function properly. In time, though, that conceptual independence was turned into a real one. What Mary Shelley offers, moreover, is a world not only in which God is absent but in which humanity takes God's place. The question of whether humanity measures up to the job is the central one of science fiction.

H. G. Wells

If Mary Shelley was pioneer of the new territory of science fiction, H. G. Wells (1866–1946) was its prime settler.[19] In four novels (*The Time Machine*, 1895; *The Island of Dr Moreau*, 1896; *The War of the Worlds*, 1898; *The First Men in the Moon*, 1901), he laid out the subject matter for most subsequent sf :[20] time travel, human social change, evolution and the end of the world; the scientist as creator, the beast-man, the lost world; alien invasion and human catastrophe; space travel and alien societies. Everywhere the theme of human 'plasticity', of our relationship with a changing cosmos is dominant.

The Island of Dr Moreau is in many ways a rewrite of *Frankenstein*. The eponymous scientist creates beast-men on an isolated island, animals reshaped as humans who chant 'laws' to embody their thin grip on civilization. As in *Frankenstein*, the scientist is full of hubris, pride, sure of his ability, undaunted by the expressed concerns of others, whilst (as there) his creations rebound on him. It is an early example of genetic manipulation, of our ability to confuse the boundaries surrounding our own identity. A modernday successor, Paul McAuley's *Fairyland* (1995), won multitudinous awards in 1996.

Wells and Jules Verne engaged in an entertaining dispute about their contrasting methods of getting their heroes to the Moon. Verne poured scorn on the antigravity substance (cavorite) that Wells used in *The First Men in the Moon*; in response Wells pointed out that Verne's gigantic propulsive gun (which he located correctly in Florida) would, upon firing a shell into space, instantaneously turn its human contents into something akin to strawberry jam.[21] Wells' travellers are inventor Cavor and entrepreneur Bedford, the latter of whom is more interested in the prospect of mineral wealth than scientific discovery. On the Moon they are captured by its inhabitants (the Selenites). Whilst Bedford escapes back to Earth, Cavor is left behind. Brought before the Selenite ruler, the Grand Lunar, he speaks too quickly of humanity's aggressive nature, and is not allowed to return. The 1964 film version had contemporary astronauts investigating the Moon discover the remains of the Selenite civilization, destroyed by germs involuntarily brought to the Moon by Cavor.

Here the film stole an idea from Wells' earlier tale of interplanetary contact, *The War of the Worlds*. It is one used in interminable subsequent stories whereby invincible aliens attempting to conquer the Earth are annihilated by the common cold. In Wells' original the Martians are moved not so much by greed as necessity, living as they do on a dying planet. For Wells, the fundamental enemies are not the Martians, horrific and remorseless as they are but the colds of space, the empty hostility of the universe whose vastness is pitted in an unequal struggle against such small oases of life as exist. This is brilliantly depicted in the scene where a survivor of the ruthless Martian assault wanders through a devastated London, hearing the dying cries of the invaders. Only as the last cry is silenced, does the terror of the situation rush in on him. Faced with a cold universe, even the alien Martians are fellow-creatures.

It is worth taking a moment here to compare a few versions of this epic tale. Of them all, the musical Jeff Wayne version (magnificently narrated by Richard Burton) is the best and truest to its original. It captures both the earthly domesticity which, for Wells, sets the scene for his unlikeliest tales and also the sheer alienness of the Martians, their incomprehensible and single-minded purpose. Its music enthralls with pity and terror as it depicts 'the beginning of the massacre of mankind'. It is humane and limitless in vision. It sees well what Wells intended, that the Martians with their enlarged gross brains and atrophied bodies represent what humanity might well become in the processes of evolution (as shown in his essay, 'The Man of the Year Million', published in 1893).

By contrast, the 1953 George Pal film is well made in terms of special effects but critically pietizes the conflict. As the Martians move in on the last human survivors of Los Angeles, praying in a crowded church, they are struck down 'by the smallest of God's creatures'. Humanity is delivered by Providence. Whilst it is true that this line is in Wells' original, there it is only a conventional piety that means nothing; more significant is the parson who goes mad. The whole point of the original book is that there is no God, no one to protect humanity; if they are saved, it is by sheer luck.

This is not the case either in the film *Independence Day* (1996), though here humanity is on its own. For all the heavily-publicized destruction and deaths of this most recent outing into alien invasion, *Independence Day* is a massively optimistic film. It celebrates the human spirit (as ably represented by America with a few token helpers) – which cannot be defeated by anyone. Even the 'virus' which defeats the aliens, though a clever concept, is one constructed by human beings.[22] The film is exhilarating, entertaining and, in the context, utterly implausible.

Wells' vision in *The War of the Worlds* is that of Darwin – evolution, the survival of the fittest, humanity alone in the universe. So too in *The Time Machine*, one of the era's great prose epics. In that story the Time Machine serves to take the traveller into two periods – one is of a distant future when humanity is divided into two halves: the peaceful, lotus-eating Eloi who live above ground and the ugly, subterranean Morlocks who prey upon them. This is a story of social and biological evolution, an evolution grounded on Victorian class divisions. It is a dreadful warning of the possible results of Disraeli's 'Two Nations'. The second period the traveller visits is more gloomy still and is what the book is *really* about: not 'a lost Eden (but) – passionately and tragically – ... the Three Laws of Thermodynamics, especially the Second'.[23] At the very end of time the traveller stands on an empty beach under a dying sun. Life on our planet is about to end. This vision of the 'End of Everything' has been very influential in science fiction. Anticipated by Shelley's *The Last Man* some sixty-nine years previously, it raises the fundamental question: if the human race becomes extinct in time, is it all for nothing?

Wells' early vision tends to the bleak. His opinion of both God (if he existed) and humanity was not high. The Selenites are quite right in wanting to prevent news of their civilization returning to Earth. As a number of sf writers observed, when celebrating the first Moon landing, 'If I were a Martian, I'd start running now!'[24] Wells asks at the beginning of *The War of the Worlds* whether, given the ruthless extinction of the Tasmanian Aborigines, we are in any position to judge the Martians in their assault on Earth.

His later work tended to be more optimistic. As well as a host of more conventional novels (like *The History of Mr Polly*, 1910), his science fiction output included a number of shorter tales like *The Invisible Man* (1897) and *The Country of the Blind* (1904) in addition to his later utopias, *The War in the Air* (1908), *The World Set Free* (1914), *Men Like Gods* (1923), *The Shape of Things to Come* (1933). These abandoned the thoughtful ambiguity of his earlier works for idealistic visions of a socialist Paradise enabled by technology. However, such utopias always emerge from fire, from an apocalyptic scenario of devastation.[25]

Conclusion

Shelley and Wells are major figures who initiated and explored central sf themes. Yet in another sense they are merely expressing a worldview, one in which God is absent from the world and in which therefore humanity has to work out its own fate alone. In so far as the Enlightenment and Romanticism express twin sides of this concentration on humanity as subject, they could be said to be the real parents of science fiction.

Chapter 4

Mirror, mirror on the wall

Few things reveal so sharply as science fiction the wishes, hopes, fears, inner stresses and tensions of an era, or define its limitations with such exactness.

(H. L. Gold)[1]

We don't need other worlds. We need a mirror. What man needs is man.

(*Solaris*)[2]

Sf desires to imagine alternate realities in order to meditate on the nature of reality. It is literally 'untrue' – fiction, not fact – yet claims in its inventions to enable a deeper understanding of reality.

Fable has always done this. James Morrow's science fiction fable, *City of Truth* (1991) envisages a world in which people are unable to lie: the result is Hell rather than Paradise. Marriages fall apart as suspicions of unfaithfulness are immediately corroborated by the culprits. A child's woodwork effort has to be described by his father as ugly and lopsided, for all that he 'sadly notes the tears welling up in his son's eyes'. A meal at the 'No Great Shakes Restaurant' – noted for the fact that its shakes are not so great! – consists of 'murdered cow sandwich, wilted hearts of lettuce and high cholesterol fries'. What this seems to prove is that truth is more than the mere equivalence of words to reality. This is corroborated by the fact that in this world there is no room for metaphor, imagination or art. The central character's job is literally that of a 'deconstructionist' art critic: his task is to smash sculptures and melt movies.

Are such things 'works of lies', though, or – as here in

40

Morrow's own madeup tale – does their fiction tell us more about the real nature of truth than any amount of purely factual reporting? The argument, therefore, is that the picturing of the other enables us to reflect on the self, the unknown on the known.

Metaphor in theory

We have already looked at the first, 'sense of wonder', theory of science fiction. The one that has come into more recent prominence is that which picks up the concerns we have just been discussing – sf as metaphor. There was always a problem with the first theory – our inherent inability to actually conceive of the genuine other, that which is really outside our experience. Unlike God, we cannot construct out of nothing because our imaginations are limited by our experience, and so we can be 'sub-creators' only (to use J. R. R. Tolkien's phrase).

Thus, classical and medieval conceptions of imaginary beasts were constructed out of existing animals: a chimera was a mixture of lion's body, goat's head and serpent's tail. David Lindsay invented two 'new' colours, jale and ulfire, in his novel, *A Voyage to Arcturus* (1920), but he could only describe them in terms of the colours we know already. The search for extraterrestrial life is hampered by our inability to imagine that which is genuinely other: how will we recognize alien life when we meet it? An entertaining running joke on the TV children's show *Sesame Street* tells this story the other way round: aliens coming to earth attempt, without success, to communicate with what they take to be its intelligent life forms. It is not their fault that ringing telephones seem to be trying to communicate with them! Similarly, Douglas Adams tells a story of an alien space fleet that is accidentally eaten by a small dog.

According to the more recent way of interpreting sf, it does not really talk about the other after all but ourselves, about other worlds but this world, about the future but the present. It acts as a barometer of changing times; it objectifies our concerns. All supposed talk of the other is really projection. Aliens are metaphors for ourselves.

The main academic proponent of this view is Darko

Suvin, a Yugoslav now teaching in Canada. He describes sf as the literature of 'cognitive estrangement'. According to him, sf is not primarily about science, the future or any specifically sf theme. It has a locale and characters which are, on the one hand, radically different from 'naturalist' fiction but, on the other, not impossible within the terms of our contemporary understanding of what we may know. This distance from accepted reality makes it potentially the space for a powerful 'estrangement'.[3] Suvin clarifies this term else-where: 'a representation which estranges (alienates) is one which allows us to recognise its subject, but at the same time makes it seem unfamiliar'.[4] Robert Scholes (a pupil of Suvin's) describes the genre, which he entitles 'structural fabulation', in a similar manner: sf is 'fiction that offers us a world clearly and radically discontinuous from the one we know, yet returns to confront that known world in some cognitive way'.[5] In other words, by postulating imaginary worlds, we are enabled to reflect on the real one and know it better.

It is important for Suvin that the mirror which he argues sf thus provides for us 'is not only a reflecting one, it is also a transforming one ... the mirror is a crucible'. It 'dynami-cally transforms' rather than simply 'statically' mirrors the world.[6] This is reminiscent of Karl Marx's saying: 'hitherto philosophers have only sought to understand the world; the point, however, is to change it' and reflects Suvin's own Marxist background.

Responses to this interpretation have been hostile in some quarters. For sf enthusiast David Hartwell, 'it is academic and therefore suspect, if not downright subversive. ... It smacks of the Academy, of the modern mythication of liter-ary energy – dry, dry, dry.'[7] For literary critic Colin Manlove, it is inadequate. 'The reasons for science fiction having become academically respectable are ... largely by being seen as a metaphor, myth or projection of our world. The science fiction medium, the range of other worlds and beings, the strange narratives and laws ... are ignored or reduced to being merely carriers – albeit commendable – of some deeper meaning that tells us more about our own condition.'[8] For him, sf does not exist simply to provide opportunities for cultural analysis: to reduce it to this disparages the sheer invention, fictional drive and longing for otherness that science fiction genuinely articulates.

According to sf critic Peter Nicholls the genre has both functions: 'to comment on our own world through the use of metaphor and extrapolation, *and* to create genuine imagined alternatives to our own world'.[9]

The reductionist approach which argues that sf is only about us can become rather dispiriting. Parts of the *Alien* film trilogy, for example, have been variously and dogmatically interpreted as about the slavery of women to their bodies, the American experience in Vietnam, and the ravages of AIDS – among other things.[10] One is alternatively bemused, impressed and (later on maybe) rather bored by the ingenuity of these approaches – if they claim to tell the whole story.[11]

Metaphor in action

For all the reservations expressed above, there is a measure of truth in the understanding of sf as telling us more about ourselves than about others. For Ursula Le Guin, science fiction can provide a metaphor for the inner life. In the 1960s writers such as J. G. Ballard coined the term 'inner space' to reflect this idea. Sf became increasingly conscious of this mirroring function.

In the classic paranoid thriller, *Invasion of the Bodysnatchers* (1956) aliens grow from pods and take over humans when they fall asleep, replacing their minds in the process. In the original ending of the film the only survivor of the first wave of invaders (with even his girfriend turning into an alien) finally manages to escape to a road, only to find lorries distributing more alien pods throughout the country. He is left in the darkness, crying to unheeding passing motorists: 'You're next! You're next!' This chilling conclusion was replaced at studio insistence by an utterly unpersuasive happy ending. The film could be (and was) seen as a McCarthyite warning of Communist subversives and infiltrators. Alternatively, it could be viewed as a satire of middle American conformism expressed in McCarthyism itself.

The Mongol-looking Klingons of 1960s *Star Trek* represented the perpetual menace of Communism. This metaphor provided the opportunity for further topical updating in changed political circumstances. *Star Trek VI* (1989) was thus a story of *glasnost*, *perestroika* and *détente* à la Gorbachev. The very transparency of the reference in many ways destroyed its force. Poul Anderson's story, 'The Helping Hand' (1951) is more subtle, showing that there is a significant difference between metaphor and allegory – the latter looking at one situation simply to refer to another; the former using a situation with its own interest to cast comment on another. In Anderson's story two planets recovering from an exhausting war seek redevelopment aid from a neutral Earth: one gratefully receives it; the other is denied it when its ambassador behaves offensively. In the second part of the story we discover the fate of the two planets. The one refused the aid has done better; forced to rely on itself through hard times, it has proudly developed its own culture. The planet that received it is doomed to touristic exploitation, economic subservience and cultural annihilation. The plot has obvious parallels with the situation of the post-World War II Marshall Plan when the United States poured financial resources into a devastated Europe. Whilst, as Kingsley Amis indicates, this story is a good example of the cognitive power of science fiction, it derives its force from the obliqueness of its reference.[12] Readers are left to add two and two together. There is a human element to the story too, one very typical of science fiction in the power it often gives the individual (but also often contrary to its ostensive message): the rejected country's ambassador is seen to have been deliberately obnoxious. Farseeing, he should have been rewarded for his actions instead of having to live in disgrace!

Less subtle is the 'Prime Directive' of *Star Trek*, 'General Order Number One', developed supposedly as an oblique criticism of the American involvement in Vietnam. In theory, the Prime Directive prohibited any interference by Starfleet with a different culture, but in practice, as has been observed, it was more honoured in the breach than in the observance – at least during the original series.[13] *Star Trek* reflected (and continues even now to reflect) the society of its time – from its original series John F. Kennedy leader (James T. Kirk: young, energetic and a womanizer) with his inspiring speeches about bringing freedom to the galaxy and exploring 'the final frontier' to its 1980s *Next Generation* New Age counsellor. The very ambiguity of its attitude to the Prime Directive can be argued to copy America's own divided mind, its certainty over the rightness of its role as global policeman combining with uncertainty as how to use its considerable power.

British sf, argues Brian Aldiss, has as one of its major ideas the theme of a 'submerged nation' which rises from ignorance or oppression to threaten its overlords.[14] The division between Eloi and Morlocks in Wells' *The Time Machine* is the model of this class division, with the sea monsters of John Wyndham's *The Kraken Awakes* (1955) and several *Dr Who* stories (Atlantean Fish People, Silurians and 'Sea Devils') less directly repeating the pattern. The sociological theme of an oppressed underclass reflects Wells' own childhood experience, brought up in an 'upstairs, downstairs' country house.[15]

By contrast American science fiction has generally concentrated on the theme of alien contact, of the other 'out there' (as in *The X-Files*). This could be argued to reflect the continuing significance of the frontier in American mythology, as well as the abiding guilt of the near-extermination of native Americans (the 'Indians' of Westerns).[16] Meanwhile, a Britain psychologically 'down' and retreating from Empire has specialized in disaster novels, from the dystopias of Huxley and Orwell to books by Wyndham, Christopher, Ballard, Aldiss, Hoyle and Hodder-Williams showing global cataclysm.[17] This is not to say that such works have been absent from the American scene; nuclear holocaust novels proliferated after World War II, making *Astounding Science Fiction* during this period rather bleak. Frederick Pohl's post-World War II short stories, full of paranoia and despairing of freedom (e.g., 'The Tunnel under the World', 1954) evidence humanity's feelings of helplessness before the power of its own creations.[18] So too perhaps the atom bomb also helped to provoke the rash of post-1945 telepathy stories: a threat of such magnitude requires a corresponding revolution in human understanding. Generally, however, the American vision was of survival, recovery and progress despite the odds.

There is a clear difference between the relentless optimism of *Star Trek* and its ilk and the satirical, cynical, anarchically-inclined British sf of writers like Terry Nation. His *Blake's Seven* (1978–81) began on television on the same day that *Star Wars* was released in the UK. Both pitted rebels against an evil Galactic Empire. *Blake's Seven* ended, however, with the utter defeat of his antiheroes, all being gunned down by the evil 'Federation' after spending four seasons inflicting mere pinpricks on it. Clute writes similarly of *Red Dwarf* (1988–) that, 'while America sent a new generation of *Star Trek* out into the populous beyond' Britain sent three no-hopers cruising vast empty reaches of empty space in a decaying ship meeting failed versions of great SF standards'.[19]

Science fiction in all countries has reflected the changing culture of its time, right through from the 'inner space' of the 1960s 'New Wave' to the postmodernist 'cyberpunk' of the 1980s and 1990s.

Prediction

Another way in which we can approach the topic of science fiction's relationship to society is in terms of the claim frequently made for it that it accurately predicts the future.

An FBI visit to *Astounding Science Fiction*'s offices in 1944, the result of a supposed security threat to the Manhattan Project posed by Cleve Cartmill's story of atomic war, 'Deadline' has been frequently singled out, particularly by its editor of the time, John W. Campbell Jnr. However, as Peter Nicholls points out, given the multitude of science fiction stories and the general level of scientific evaluation among its writers, the odds of a few hits among the misses are reasonable. 'For every correct prediction a dozen were wrong, or correct only if facts were stretched a little.'[20]

Almost all of the sf stories of the 1950s had humanity's first journey to the Moon achieved by free enterprise, with Heinlein's *Rocket Ship Galileo* (1947) the most extreme – being largely constructed by teenage boys in a backyard! This vision reflected the beloved entrepreneurial culture of Edison with a large dose of wishful thinking thrown in. Not a single one of the thousands of stories published about the first landing of human beings on the moon proposed another of the most singular of its aspects, notably that it would be shown worldwide on television. Similarly, a science fiction that has concentrated on intelligent robots and sentient androids has failed to predict the enormous increase in personal computers and the vast array of easily accessible worldwide information. For every success – like Arthur C. Clarke's proposing of communication satellites – there have been many failures.

Nor has success been more evident in the social realm. The impact of feminism in the Western world has given rise to revolutionary changes to language and behaviour. Yet feminist science fiction has accompanied rather than preceded change: sf has reflected the mores of its age. Only a few stories stand out – John Wyndham's 'Consider Her Ways and Others' (1956) is a tale of a female-only society in which men have been rendered unnecessary; this is now a common idea. Even the widely respected Ursula K. Le Guin finds in her early works (like *The Left Hand of Darkness*, 1969) an unconsidered acceptance of patriarchal structures which she now wants to leave behind.[21] Those aspects of *Star Trek* which were forward-looking in its time – namely a (relatively) egalitarian crew, with gender and racial representation (for example, Uhura as a black woman officer) – represented the liberal hopes (and even practices) of the time. (They were, of course, not insignificant. Nichelle Nicholls, who played Uhura – the Swahili word for 'freedom' – is fond of relating how Martin Luther King told her she could not leave the show when she was feeling disenchanted with it: she was just too important a role model for blacks.)[22]

Science fiction stories of the kind we have been discussing are essentially extrapolations, guesses of what might happen in the future on the basis of what we know already. Most such extrapolations are notoriously unreliable. As David Brin points out, very often we simply do not know what is already happening in our society at a significant level, let alone what the future will bring.[23] Hiroshima was one event that science fiction writers claim to have understood better than anyone else[24] – but they had been thinking about it, or something like it for a long time. On the other hand, the abrupt collapse of Communism in Eastern Europe and the USSR in the late 1980s and early 1990s was anticipated by almost nobody. Stories set several hundred years into a future which featured a still dominantly communist USSR expanding into the Stars in wary co-operation with the capitalists (as in Larry Niven and Jerry Pournelle's *The Mote in God's Eye*, 1974) were left looking rather silly. Overall one is left feeling rather sceptical of the predictive powers of science fiction.

One serious extrapolative sf novel is David Brin's *Earth* (1990), dedicated to 'Our Common Mother' and clearly designed to raise ecological awareness. In the context of wide-sweeping alterations in geography, society and economics (widespread flooding, endemic skin cancer, mass animal extinctions and so forth), Christianity and other religions have been eclipsed by ecological devotion to Gaia (the Earth) and Ra (the Sun).

Is this plausible? In the longer term, maybe. The novel, however, is set in 2038, barely forty years from now. The general tendency to exaggerate has been a repeated problem with futurology – as with all apocalyptic prophecies of the Jehovah's Witness variety. The world of the film *Blade Runner* is set in the Los Angeles of the year 2019, yet today we see no sign of the out-world colonies, let alone androids, it depicts. Arthur C. Clarke's *2001: A Space Odyssey* posits intelligent thinking machines like the HAL 9000 computer series, as well as vast orbiting space stations, regular transit shuttles to the moon, and the capacity to send vast space-ships to Jupiter. None of these are even remotely on the drawing board as yet.

Perspective

In a recent book, physicist Carl Sagan argued that the 1990 view back from interplanetary probe *Voyager 2* as it left the solar system enabled us to see ourselves as inhabitants of an (ever-diminishing) 'pale blue dot', a sight that was 'humbling'. Opined Sagan, there is 'no better a demonstration of the folly of human conceits' – our wars revealed as no more than 'the squabbling of mites on a plum'. A *Time* review concluded that Sagan had 'placed Earth in proper perspective'.

Sf, too, claims to put humanity 'in proper perspective', to have access to an Olympian viewpoint, one transcending the 'petty squabbles' of humans on this planet. Methodologically, however, this assertion is problematic – since, once again, it is we who are the ones writing and dreaming the sf. Harlan Ellison may claim that sf gives us a 'view from a distant star', but this is basically a conjuring trick of misdirection.[25] Olaf Stapledon's deliberately 'objectivist' philosophy is as partisan, committed and subjective as any other – and even more dangerous for being bogus enough to claim not to be.

Thinking about the claim to perspective, then, we reach the same conclusion as we did when discussing those of prediction and alienness. Neither the genuinely alien, the genuinely new nor the genuinely distant perspective can be produced by science fiction for all its trying. There is a lot of fun in sf and rightly so, but let us not pretend that it has a true purchase on reality. When it does that, the genre becomes pompous, as in the 1996 BBC TV series, *Future Fantastic*, which made extravagant claims for the predictive abilities of the genre.

What we have been doing in this chapter is to identify some of the limitations of sf. In the next we shall go on to look at what sf enthusiasts have made of the genre themselves.

Chapter 5

Enlightenment: disciples of the new religion

Most science fiction is to authentic scientific, philosophical, or theological knowledge as pornography is to love. . . . Science fiction does not convey to me the fate of man strapped in his own devices but rather removes itself from human concerns through deceptive ballyhoo.

(Stanislaw Lem)[1]

The names in science fiction are mere labels – Gagarin, Glenn – symbols, heroic labels, names of astronauts. The humanity of the astronaut is a liability, a weakness, irrelevant to his mission. As astronaut, he is not a being: he is an act. It is the act that counts. We are in the age of Science, where nothing *is*. None of the scientists, none of the philosophers, can say what anything or anyone is. They can only say, accurately, beautifully, what it does. The age of Technology; of Behaviourism; the age of the Act.

(Ursula Le Guin)[2]

Sf and character: criticisms from within

Strange as it may seem, some of the most scathing criticisms of science fiction come from within the genre, by people whose works have been honoured and admired by many in it. Their words are, nevertheless, often savage. Some, such as cult US author Kurt Vonnegut, have tried to distance themselves from membership of the 'lodge'.[3] After all, sf has not only been ghettoized: it has ghettoized itself. Those daring to criticize science fiction may get into trouble: the Polish writer Stanislaw Lem's honorary membership of the SFWA (Science Fiction Writers of America) was withdrawn in

1976 after he had described most sf as a 'cultural cancer'! (Ironically, Lem is regarded as the best sf candidate for a literary Nobel.)[4] If 'mainstream' literature has tended to look down on science fiction, very often too sf has looked down on mainstream literature with the fervour of those who believe they are prophesying the millennium. Sf fans are, in their own eyes, harbingers of the only literature worth writing. This is thus not just a ghetto mentality, but a messianic one too. In this chapter we will examine what Edward James has called 'the sf community'.[5] James plausibly argues the importance of sf fans compared to the enthusiasts of other literary genres. In their hardcore form, they represent a true self-declared élite.

As we have already observed, sf has not always been sectarian. In the UK writers such as Doris Lessing, Kingsley Amis, Angus Wilson and P. D. James still produce what some call 'non-genre science fiction'. Nevertheless, the general attitude of 'mainstream' literature to science fiction has tended to be disparaging, especially over the past forty years or so. 'Mainstream' critics question the literary qualities of sf: its plot construction, characterization, colourfulness, style, credibility and human insight. Lem agrees with them at this point, differentiating between two forms of literature, an upper realm (mainstream fiction) and a lower realm (trivial literature). He argues that science fiction belongs to the lower realm and this can be easily proved. Most sf is written rapidly and read only once. Most sf readers are almost wholly unable to differentiate a good from a poor piece of writing.[6] Sf authors work at the dictates of their publishers, who determine the title, length and content of their stories.

Yet sf does not readily acknowledge or accept this state, continues Lem: it has pretensions which go far beyond. 'If we may believe its claims, a science fiction book belongs at the top of world literature. For it reports on mankind's destiny, and the meaning of life in the cosmos, on the rise and fall of thousand year old civilisations; it brings forth a deluge of answers for the key questions of every reasoning being.'[7] All this despite the extraordinary speed and lack of precision of its million-word rambling tales! For Lem, then, sf is mostly marked by triviality and pretension.

Ursula Le Guin is one of two modern authors approved of by Lem. (The other is Philip K. Dick, ironically noted for how fast he wrote his works!) Le Guin's own views on sf are expressed in the essay, 'Science Fiction and Mrs Brown', which takes as its starting point twentieth-century English novelist Virginia Woolf's own meditation about a real person once observed by her in a railcarriage, a person she dubs 'Mrs Brown'. Woolf writes of the end of her encounter that, as Mrs Brown marched away into Waterloo station, 'she looked very small, very tenacious, at once very frail and very heroic'. For Woolf, 'all novels begin with an old lady in the corner opposite'. Le Guin asks crucially whether the small heroic figure of Mrs Brown can be accommodated in science fiction:

> Have we any hope of catching Mrs Brown, or are we trapped for good inside our great, gleaming spaceships hurtling out across the galaxy, antiseptic vehicles moving faster than the Richmond–Waterloo train, faster than the speed of light, ships capable of containing heroic captains in black and silver uniforms, and second officers with peculiar ears, and mad scientists with nubile daughters, ships capable of blasting other, inimical ships into smithereens with their apocalyptic, holocaustic rayguns, and of bringing loads of colonists from Earth to unknown worlds inhabited by incredibly sinister or beautiful forms of alien life, ships capable of anything, absolutely anything, except one thing: they cannot contain Mrs Brown. She simply doesn't fit.[8]

This argument makes essentially the same point as Lem: sf's emphasis on size fails to see what is really important genuine human reality. In one striking *Star Trek: The Next Generation* tale, 'Family', Captain Jean-Luc Picard returned to his parents' house in France, having had both his body and mind taken over by alien androids called the Borg. He is wounded in mind and spirit. The story climaxes with Picard wrestling in the mud with his apparently obnoxious brother (brilliantly played by Jeremy Kemp). As Picard dissolves into tears and admits his vulnerability, it is suddenly extraordinarily difficult to take seriously the stainless steel world of the *Enterprise* supposedly orbiting the planet several miles above. 'Family' was the first *Star Trek* episode without a scene on the bridge of the *Enterprise*: perhaps this is why it was also the lowest-rated of the season.[9] It is genuinely moving. The question, however, is whether human reality 'fits' into sf. Or, as Le Guin says, if starships do not have room for Mrs Brown (or, rather, if Mrs Brown is too *large* to be encompassed by the limited scope of science fiction), then she has no interest in science fiction.

Sf in its turn has mixed reaction to Le Guin's comments. Although her work is held in high regard in the sf community, most have thought her criticism unjustified. As she acknowledges, the novel of character that is her model is the product of modern post-Enlightenment, middle-class Europe. So too it has been argued that so-called realistic literature (that is, literature that teaches you 'about life') is only one form of it, and may itself be questioned for its presuppositions. The belief that the truth about the human self is to be gained by introspective self-analysis is dubious for some. Virginia Woolf's claim that, 'Mrs Brown is eternal, Mrs Brown is human nature' is disputed by those for whom the notion of eternal human nature is a myth. H. G. Wells argued against Henry James that a close scrutiny of character is possible only when the social frame remains constant. Sf analyses the frame which change has made part of the picture. It thus gives a wider perspective.[10]

The vast majority of science fiction relegates character to minor significance: other things – plot, place, theme, idea – are primary. The centrality of idea to sf means that stories frequently sound good in paraphrase. For C. S. Lewis, this is good: the absence of intense characterization is required for the genre to function. If the situation is strange, to have peculiar people as well would be 'an oddity too much'.[11] The very ordinariness of Wells' characters (for example, Cavor and Bedford in *The First Men in the Moon*) is not a demerit but a virtue. Thus they can represent humanity in general, with reactions typical of us all.

Isaac Asimov's stories are classic examples of bare characterization and uncomplicated prose. Some sf writing styles are excruciating – none, surely, as bad as E. E. 'Doc' Smith's in his *Lensman* series. More profoundly problematic, though, for Le Guin is the fact that in none of the galaxies, planets, robots, technologies, evolution to Godhead, stars,

> are there any people. There is Humanity, and After, as in Stapledon. There is Inhumanity, and After, as in Orwell and Huxley. There are captains and troopers, and aliens and maidens and scientists, and emperors and robots and monsters – all signs, all symbols, statements, effigies, allegories, everything between the Stereotype and the Archetype. But not Mrs Brown.[12]

She argues that the unimportance of particular names in science fiction indicates that it does not deal with the unique but with the standard, the representative. Humanity in general is the topic of sf – as in the fictional Laws of Psychohistory developed by Isaac Asimov for his *Foundation* series (to go with the famous 'Three Laws of Robotics' to which Le Guin caustically alludes above). It is significant that Asimov's Laws do not cater for the individual (thus the disruptive effect of the mutant 'Mule' in *Foundation and Empire*), but rather deal with the predictable mass.

Dick vs. Asimov: the individual and reason

To analyse this and other tendencies in sf further, let us contrast Asimov's work with that of Philip K. Dick. Both are popular writers. Dick is the hero in Lem's essay, 'Science fiction: a hopeless case – with exceptions'. (He is the exception: 'A Visionary among the Charlatans'. Nobody could accuse Lem of pulling his punches.) Dick's characters are unexceptional too, but they are heroic in their very ordinariness – 'the ordinary Joe' (Joe Chip in *Ubik*, Joe Timbane in *Counter-Clock World*, Jack Bohlen in *Martian Time-Slip*, Tagomi in *The Man in the High Castle*). They inhabit a moral universe, thus fulfilling Virginia Woolf's requirements. The science fiction setting, the paraphernalia of exotic sets and so forth are wheeled out as much by Dick as by anyone, but in order to investigate fundamental problems, not for their own sake. In *Ubik* (1969) the world is disintegrating: the plot surrounds the attempts of the main character to discover even if he is alive. In *Flow my Tears, The Policeman Said* (1974) the main character is translated to a world in which he is unknown and does not seem to exist. *The Man in the High Castle* (1962) and *Martian Time-Slip* (1964) deal with parallel worlds, and our ability to create our own reality, *Do Androids Dream of Electric Sheep* (1968) with rogue android 'replicants' pursued by bounty-hunters ('blade-runners' in the Ridley Scott film adaptation). In all these, stock science fiction ideas are used, but unlike, say, Larry Niven's *Ringworld* (1970), they are not the centre of the story. Instead, the moral dilemmas of the characters are.

In *Counter-Clock World* (1967) time has begun to run backwards – as in the *Red Dwarf* episode of this title. People begin their lives by being dug up from their graves and taken to hospital to recover from their fatal illnesses, after which they become progressively younger. Eventually, they regress into the womb and finally into nothingness as a willing couple engages in sexual intercourse. The ideas are self-contradictory though entertaining (for example, food that has to be disgorged and then returned to packets, clothes that have to be put on dirty, and so forth). This, however is not the point: rather, moral dilemmas are. Adultery, black-mail and murder predominate: sin is a valid word to use in this book, a word which by itself separates Dick's work from most science fiction.

Isaac Asimov (also known as the 'Dean of sf') is, by contrast, a good example of several tendencies in science fiction – its general lack of human depth or any interest in the intricacies of human psychology, its intellectualism, its concentration on plot and idea. Asimov's stories are very often in the detec-tive-story vein. They have bizarre and cunning plot twists which beguile the reader into the wrong line of thinking, until the author finally reveals both the answer and his own cleverness.

The heroes of Asimov's stories are models of rationality, clarity and objectivity. They are self-possessed, confident and analytic, and react 'calmly' rather than 'emotionally' to events. They have neat, tidy and productive minds – like Asimov's own. It has been suggested that Asimov approves of robots precisely because of this rationality. Any deficiencies they may exhibit in his stories are almost always the result of human error. They are thus become for him suitable guardians for the human race, and indeed take on that role in his later *Foundation* novels.

Asimov's stories are also noticeable for their lack of sense of place. Of his galaxy-famous city of Trantor we get the most bare description. Action zips across the light years but new star systems are merely the key to a new intellectual puzzle. One of his works is evocatively titled *The Stars Like Dust* (1951), but its content is prosaic in the extreme.

The rationalism so evident in Asimov is critiqued by Philip K. Dick. Dick follows Dostoyevsky's view that 'the danger of man's self-destruction [lies] not in his failure to control the irrational but in his denial of its existence and his adulation of the rational'.[13] The intelligent, emotionless robots that figure repeatedly in Dick's fiction (notably *Do Androids Dream of Electric Sheep*) act as metaphors for human rationality drained of empathy. They are dangerous. They have 'something a bit chilly about them, like a breath from the vacuum between inhabited worlds, in fact from nowhere'.[14] The theme of the nature of the authentically human – as opposed to that which only masquerades as human – was a continued concern of Dick, as shown in his two essays: 'The Android and the Human' (1972) and 'Man, Android and Machine' (1976). Enough exists to show us that Dick's viewpoint is drastically different, if not directly opposed, to Asimov's. By contrast with Asimov's apparent unbridled optimism about a technological future, Dick breathes scepticism: scepticism as to the nature of reality, to the possibility of our knowledge of it, and, moreover, to 'the estrangements of technological societies'.[15] But despite the uncertainties and never-ending webs of illusion in Dick's novels, what *is* unwavering is his moral sensibility. He recognizes and portrays the actuality of evil: 'a kind of being, lacking in empathy, sympathy or any sense of common humanity – be it android, psychotic, junkie, autistic, paranoid or fascist'.[16] This applies not only to the androids of *Do Androids Dream of Electric Sheep* but also to the Nazis of *The Man in the High Castle* and the flawed Gnostic subdeity of *The Three Stigmata of Palmer Eldritch* (1965).

Sf in general follows Asimov against Dick. Does this stress on rationality in sf witness to its adolescent beginnings – and that period's typical fear of emotion and the particular? Asimov often has a lonely outcast as hero. Such people are finding their feet, discovering their place in the world, conscious of their individuality and (mostly) defiant. But how genuine is Asimov's espousal of rationality anyway? His own favourite story was the emotional anti-science 'The Ugly Little Boy' (1958).[17] Is that 'scientific impersonalness' a fraud? His favourite character is a robotpsychologist, the icy Susan Calvin: could it be that her combination of misanthropy and ferocious concern for 'her' robots is the result of extreme loneliness?

One might add that while most of Asimov's work reveals unequivocal and unbridled enthusiasm for the future, his personal responses do not. Interviewed in 1969, Asimov embarked on a catalogue of present and possible dangers to humanity and our planet familiar to any eco-doom monger.[18] Apart from odd hints in works like *The Gods Themselves* (with its suggestive section titles: 'Against Stupidity', 'The Gods Themselves', 'Contend in Vain?') his own writing has not reflected this. His last works returned nostalgically (and very lucratively) to the world of the Foundation and Robots. In his very last novel his hero, Hari Seldon (increasingly an *alter ego*) is married to a robot: her 'death' is actually quite moving. Moreover, actual individuals are not only important but actually vital for Asimov – even in books supposedly dedicated to the opposite premise ('the inevitability of history'). In Asimov's seminal *Foundation* series only the action of one woman, Bayta Darrell, prevents the destruction of Hari Seldon's dream, whatever Asimov's doubletalk to the contrary.

The kind of psychological analysis (reductionism, maybe) I have embarked upon above is anathema to many science fiction fans – and with some justification. Yet Asimov may be taken as representative of many fans themselves. As John Clute and Malcolm Edwards have said, his was the 'default' voice of science fiction for five decades.[19] His emphases on problem-solving, plot rather than style, idea rather than character are typical of much science fiction.

The Golden Age

How far then does Asimov represent 'the Golden Age' of
science fiction – not the era of the 40s and 50s but the era
of adolescence? As David Hartwell has put it, 'the Golden
Age of science fiction is twelve'. Adolescence is a time of
change, which sf deals with above all. The caricature of the sf
fan is a pimply young male, uncertain in identity and anxious
about his relations with the opposite sex. He reacts to criticism
with undiscriminating enthusiasm and blinkered self-right-
eousness. It could be argued that the emotional immaturity
of the age is reflected in the fear and inexperience which are
sublimated into objectivization in the manner of Asimov.
Science fiction's concentration on the general rather than the
particular, on the race rather than the individual makes it
'safer' to handle – for all its grandiose claims. Such an age has
an idealism which may be difficult to temper but easy to shape
into distant 'causes' – whether it be the fate of the whales or
humanity's 'outward urge'. Science fiction is typically impersonal. The classic science fiction hero is the lonely thinker:
sf celebrates 'brains rather than brawn'. The TV series *Dr
Who* used to perpetuate this concept with its emphasis on the
scientist doctor as saviour, as opposed to the blundering
action-orientated soldiers (like the Brigadier) who were
regarded with a kind of affectionate contempt.[20]

Such emphases could slide into a kind of scientistic tech-
nocracy, seeing sf fans as the brainy ones who really run the
world, or ought to. This was partially because others might
sneer at them as 'four-eyes' or 'eggheads'. Enthusiast Donald
Wollheim wrote that, 'the normal science fiction devotee
tends to be solitary and introverted in his youth. . . . Reading
it exclusively can be as compulsive as a narcotic for a period
of an intelligent teenager's life.'[21] Sf's very detachment from
issues of personal relationships can make it attractive, whilst
feeding a pride in intellect and the feeling of belonging to
an élite who really know the truth about the world. One
thirteen year old wrote to an sf magazine complaining of his
school teacher whose distaste for science fiction showed that
she was 'one of those people who have a closed mind'. The
fact that he was 'a big fan of Asimov and Heinlein' revealed,

by contrast, that he was one of those 'more advanced human beings, who possess more open minds and know better'. The magazine congratulated the writer for his perspicacity.[22]

In this way of thinking, it can be argued that the lost child of science fiction was rewarded for his loneliness through the 'power fantasies' of the genre he loved, fantasies which dwelt upon the beginning and end of man (conceived impersonally). It constructed galactic civilizations, was full of intellectual puzzles about abstract ideas and had titles like 'Stimulus' and 'The Mother of Invention'.

Much treatment of ESP (extra-sensory perception) falls into this category. Instead of mile-long spaceships and galaxy-spanning empires, we find supermen able to raise spaceships with a thought (as in *Star Wars*) or to communicate with others by use of the mind alone. (*Independence Day*, of course, has *500* kilometre spaceships *and* telepathy!) Such concepts dominated the *Astounding Science Fiction* of the mid-1950s.

More than any other work, Theodore Sturgeon's *More than Human* (1953) expresses the loneliness of the outsider, persecuted by 'normal' people, and incomprehensible to them. It is a moving and beautifully written book. The development of the super-human is associated with the problem of how to deal with 'ordinary' people. The book argues that what appears to be a curse is really a blessing – the talents which make the outsiders different and persecuted are the key to a new stage in human evolution. Experiences of suffering at the hands of 'normals' generate compensatory assertions of superiority and a desire for revenge, but they should be resisted. The extent to which such books act as metaphors for a self-conscious scientific intellectual group seems clear. Throughout we feel the idea of alienation from society. It is hardly surprising that science fiction breeds élitism. In numerous works (A. E. Van Vogt's *Slan*, 1940; book 1946; Henry Kuttner's *Mutant*, 1953; and John Wyndham's *Re-Birth*, 1955) the theme of the persecuted emergent race has been repeated. In other variations of the theme, it is the scientist who, following a worldwide apocalypse – generally of the nuclear variety – is discriminated against and has to work with difficulty to survive and guard the rest of an ungrateful human race.[23]

For some this reflects intellectual maturity (or at least knowledge) without accompanying emotional or spiritual capacity – a kind of spiritual adolescence. This could be paralleled with the position of the human race in the late twentieth century – armed with weapons of mass destruction and apparently without the ability to restrain itself from using them.

If 'twelve' (or 'thirteen'!) has its drawbacks, it has its merits too. Above all, it is an energetic and enthusiastic age. It has a confidence in itself that has to be welcomed ('We can do better!'), even if it appears naive to the eyes of experience. It tends to be unmaterialistic, not being interested in personal success, in 'getting on'. There is a wonder at the universe and discontent at aspects perceived to be wrong with it – and a desire to put them right. *Star Trek*'s much commented-on optimism reflects much of this age's attitude – along with a certain anxiety and fear of failure. Wesley Crusher in *Star Trek: The Next Generation* (a much loathed figure to some fans – 'a child on the bridge of the *Enterprise!*') was said by *Star Trek* creator Gene Roddenberry to portray himself (Wesley was his middle name).[24] Wesley represented in many ways humanity itself, fledgeling and making mistakes – but learning, discovering, keen to go 'where no one has gone before'. He thus represents the inquisitiveness of youth faced with a universe vaster and more interesting than remotely imagined. The 'wolfling', dynamic humanity of David Brin's space opera *Startide Rising* (1983) is in precisely the same vein: precociously, Earth refuses to be sat upon by elder, wiser and more powerful races and, in so doing, becomes the saviour of the galaxy.

The youthful energy of science fiction represents a confident, expanding outlook. It can be argued to be typically American, being contrasted by some (in the manner of William James) with the backward-looking decrepitude of Europe. For Greg Bear, science fiction with its outward and future bent represents the ideal of the USA.[25] Science fiction is thus the expression of the 'new frontier', of the excitement of the space age, of humanity reaching the Moon, of going beyond its place of birth to expand through the universe.

There is in science fiction a certain youthful innocence, contrasted with the experience of age.

Pushing the envelope

Many of the criticisms of sf stem from within the genre, as the swingeing assaults by Lem and Le Guin reveal. There may be those who wish to impose a party line, but since the genre itself stands for imaginative dreaming, this is stiffly resisted. For author Thomas M. Disch class issues are significant. If, as he believes, sf expresses the resentment and power fantasies of an emerging semi-literate working class audience (compensated for its actual lack of power in the real world), he does not believe this is necessarily a bad thing: 'fantasies of power are a necessary prerequisite to its exercise. . . . Personal virtue and the magic of machines counterbalance in sf the inherited wealth and corresponding control exercised by the ruling classes.'[26] Such resentment may appear in ludicrously immature and paranoid form: in A. E. Van Vogt's *The World of Null-A* (1948), lack of education is argued to be an advantage in solving problems: the so-called authorities are a pack of fools and frauds with minds closed to any but their own ideas.

Here we return to the thirteen year old American boy's opinion of school and its teachers, and his proud allegiance to a genre whose adherents, as Disch says, 'regard their involvement as a badge of intellectual distinction, like a membership in MENSA'. Hence what he sees as the 'fascism lurking beneath the smooth chromium surface of a good deal of science fiction. . . . Fan, after all, is a shortened form of fanatic.'[27]

Chapter 6

Science and religion
Part one: escape from religion

Extinguished theologians lie about the cradle of every science
as the strangled snakes beside that of Hercules.

(T. H. Huxley)[1]

Of course it is not arrogant to ask those questions: 'Who are
we? Where do we come from? Why are we this way and not
some other?' They may be difficult to answer, but if scientists
cannot answer them it is certain that nobody else can.

(Richard Dawkins)[2]

Conceptual breakthrough

Sf tends to combine a high view of science's revelatory role
with a low one of any other method. Its general hostility to
Christianity is given expression in a series of stories which
use the tropes of the genre with ingenuity. In particular the
'generation starship' tale (so called because the space trip will
last for generations because of the vast interstellar distances
involved) gives the opportunity to pour ridicule on traditional
religion and portray it as ignorance cloaked in piety. The
scenario provides an ideal locale to poke fun at a blinkered,
ignorant society, the way it is maintained and the way it
might be broken. Typically in such stories, the ship's original
location or purpose has been forgotten by its crew over the
period of time.[3] The nature of the ship is misunderstood and
its contents thought to be the whole universe.

Robert Heinlein's significantly entitled story, 'Universe'

(1941) is one of the seminal works of the subgenre. In it, 'Manning Landing Stations' has come to be thought of as 'a purely religious ceremony' and the language of 'Earth', 'the Ship' and 'our heavenly home, Centaurus' (the intended colony) are thought to be mythology. Scientific texts are interpreted spiritually: 'the law of Gravitation' in *Basic Modern Physics* is demythologized as an allegory of the mutual attraction of human love!

Science brings salvation from this mire. The climax of the story occurs when a boy sees the true universe from the ship's Control Room. 'He knew, subconsciously, that having seen the stars he would never be happy again. The dull ache in his breast, the vague inchoate yearning for his last heritage of open sky and stars was never to be silenced.'[4] The literal (and metaphorical) undoing of the shutters is the moment of epiphany, of enlightenment. Even when condemned to death by his scientist superiors for heresy, he declares in the legendary defiant words of Galileo: 'Nevertheless, it still moves!'

For Heinlein, not all will hear the call. In an almost Calvinist sense revelation (for that is what we are talking about) will be denied by many: they are doomed, and in Heinlein's opinion deservedly. In a successor to this story, 'Common Sense', the majority, 'hopelessly blinded by "common sense" are not converted but abandoned. The ship is left to continue its benighted path; the small band of visionaries goes off to begin a new existence on a virgin planet.'[5]

The idea of 'conceptual breakthrough' is central. If in Heinlein's tale, the stars are redemptive, in Asimov's 'Nightfall' – often described as sf's most famous story – (also 1941) they are damning. When every 21,049 years five of the six suns set and the sixth is eclipsed, the unimaginable grandeur of the planet's position in the midst of a globular star cluster is revealed. Madness sets in and the cities burn. It is indicative of sf's high vision of the heavens that, although beholding them provokes destruction, it is their glory that does so.

James Blish's 'Surface Tension' (1952) tells the story of humans miniaturized to survive on a remote planet who forget their origins and have to discover a greater world – by sending a machine to leave the puddle in which they have been living! The popularity of this story puzzled Blish for many years. Darko Suvin explained it to him with a magazine cover, which depicted a medieval monk crawling out of the familiar world of the Aristotelian spheres and looking amazedly at the totally different universe he finds outside them. 'That is what most of your serious work is about', he announced.[6] As in Heinlein's stories, this contrasts rationalist science with obscurantist religion.

The immoralities of religion

The model of the unrelieved war to the death between science and religion is shown by repeated stories. It is along these lines that Kingsley Amis wrote:

> When the sun seems about to turn into a nova, when the alien space fleet closes in, when famine and pestilence follow in the wake of a nuclear war, prophets and fanatics impose themselves on the rabble while the scientists set their jaws and get on with the job. . . . Organised religion among alien subject peoples is to be treated, when possible, with the same sort of respect as their dietary habits, but will probably come in handy if taken over and used as a means of manipulating them.[7]

H. Beam Piper follows this pattern in his 'Temple Trouble' stories, which have 'Paratime Police' operating under the cover of priests. Such stories developed the notion that religions might be useful – so long as they are entirely insincere (a belief also found in Asimov's *Foundation* series). The history of the Church has unfortunately provided critics with lots of targets to aim at and Terry Pratchett's *Small Gods* (1992) hits them all unerringly. The cover of the book, showing a naked victim being tortured by the Exquisitors ('like Inquisitors, only worse'), sums up Pratchett's Enlightenment view of religion – highly dangerous, self-deceiving and the purveyor of misery. Religious wars extend oppression and absurdity; religion is the curse of humankind.

Disposing of Jesus

Jesus himself can be disposed of in many ways. In Arthur C.
Clarke's 'The Star' (1955) his birth is signalled by a super-
nova that destroys alien civilizations, causing a spiritual crisis
for a space-travelling priest who discovers this centuries in
the future. In Michael Moorcock's *Behold the Man* (1966) a
modern time-traveller seeking the historic Christ becomes
Jesus and is crucified – an idea repeated in several stories. In
Philip José Farmer's wordy *Riverworld* series (1965–83), a
dazed 'Yeshua' is reincarnated on an alien planet.[8] Alfred
Bester's *Extro* (1975) sees 'Jacy' (i.e., J. C.) as the immortal
Wandering Jew, still talking about the 'wild surprise of death
that shocked through him on the cross when he finally
realised he was not going to be rescued by the US Marines'.[9]
Endless are the games science fiction can play with the
'Founder of Christianity'.

Arthur C. Clarke has a special animosity for what he
regards as life-destroying Christianity. In his *The Fountains
of Paradise* (1979) an extraterrestrial spaceship entering the
solar system is 'unfortunately' interrogated by radio. When
Aquinas' *Summa* is fed to it, it is demolished briefly with 'a
list of 192 fallacies'! By the time the ship leaves the solar
system, Clarke writes, it has 'put an end to the billions of
words of pious gibberish with which apparently intelligent
men had addled their minds for centuries'.[10]

In Heinlein's 'Future History' we meet a theocratic tyran-
ny run by a rabble-rousing demagogue, Nehemiah Scudder,
in Blish's equivalent the equally ruthless use of electronic
evangelism by 'Believers'. In the future Christianity will either
become fanatical or die out completely.[11] Stories dealing with
alien religions or societies may be more sympathetic than
those picturing Christianity – as in *Deep Space Nine*'s (1993–)
treatment of Bajoran mystical religion reveals. *Babylon 5*'s
(1993–) respectful treatment of Christianity as an ally against
the forces of evil is an exception – as in many things for this
innovative series.[12]

James Blish's *A Case of Conscience* (1958) postulates an
apparently sinless alien race posing problems for yet another
priest.[13] Priests, especially devout Jesuit ones, are popular

foils of threats to faith and one appears yet again in Dan
Simmons' epic *Hyperion Cantos* (1990). Here, as one of the
last members of an almost extinct Christianity, he is the victim
of an organic parasitical cruciform which attaches itself to
his chest and renders him effectively immortal. He ends up
being crucified, perpetually dying in agony, perpetually being
reborn.[14] Sf typically uses such speculations in an attempt to
fictively refute Christianity – a sleight of hand which is both
dishonest and common. The general view is that 'religious
commitment of any kind is superstition maintained by the
self-interested fraudulence of a ruling power'.[15]

Apes and cavemen

The past in sf is usually read as a slow climb from barbarism
– thus Wells' and Clarke's 'Dawn of Man' tales.[16] Sf both celebrates evolution and indicts the ignorance it thinks would
refuse it (thus the brilliantly ironic *Planet of the Apes*, 1963,
with intelligent orang-utans denying that humans could be
made in the image of God!).

Other variations on the 'apes and cavemen' theme have
included William Golding's *The Inheritors* (1955). This
deliberately turns on its head Wells' thesis of barbaric
Neanderthals being supplanted by more advanced Cro-
Magnons; rather, the newcomers are the barbaric ones,
ruthless and violent, destroying without pity the sensitive,
artistic Neanderthal culture. Many others – like Jean
Auel – have shown both fascination and sympathy for our
remote ancestors. Concentration on them has enabled some
reflection on what we are ourselves.

Works like James Blish's *Doctor Mirabilis* (1964), Harry
Turtledove's *Agent of Byzantium* (1987) and Paul McAuley's
Pasquale's Angel (1994) are forays into the Middle Ages, the
latter two an alternate one. For all their scholarship, they succeed more in celebrating nascent evidence of technology than
in understanding the religious milieu. This is not unexpect-
ed for, in virtually all sf, science is seen as the saving element
of history past and future. Those who oppose it, for whatever
reason, are the opponents of humanity and, depending on
the nobility of the author, may be disposed of accordingly.

Memories

Conceptual breakthrough is often expressed in terms of the uncovering of former wisdom. Such an emphasis is, at first glance, strange for a genre stressing the new. It seems to place the reader more with the medieval Christian rediscovering the legacy of the pagan past (the Renaissance reaffirmation of classical Greece and Rome) than with modern humanity or even the Enlightenment of the eighteenth century.

As we have seen, origins in generation starship stories are often depicted as having been forgotten, mythicized or given supernatural explanation. Whole races are also shown as having lost their beginnings, whilst inheriting intriguing, if saddening, fragments of previous achievements (thus Larry Niven's 'The Soft Weapon', 1967, Charles Sheffield's *Heritage*, 1990–, and David Brin's *Uplift* series, 1980–, and the *Star Trek* concept of 'the Preservers'[17]).

In all this we see an emphasis on knowledge as remembering. According to this model, humans are the inheritors of something much greater than they think – but they have forgotten who they are and where they came from. In this model, we are indeed 'stardust', golden beings whose origins are near (if not actually) divine. In an ancient Greek Orphic myth humanity was descended from the blood of a god killed by Zeus. In the Romanticism both of the nineteenth century and of hippy pop lyrics the same theme is repeated. Even in modern astronomy we are reminded that were it not for the violent explosion of supernovae in the early universe the higher elements such as iron would not exist. As the 'Stardust' episode of *The Astronomers* TV series put it: 'we are born in stars . . . we are such things as dreams are made on'.

This concept of remembering (*anamnesis* in Greek) is crucial to both sf and Greek culture. Fredericks argues that 'Greek myths seem peculiarly appropriate as myths and metaphors to be used in sf since they were developed in a rational and speculative culture.'[18] Rationality (or rationalism) and myth go together in both cases. Sf thrives on stories ('myths') of human origin and destiny. The motif of remembering where one has come from, indeed that one is the descendent of a far greater past, is one of the most central of these. Here, then, there is a clue to science fiction's similarity to the ancient Christian heresy of Gnosticism that we shall discuss further in the next chapter.

The modernist dream

'What they've done is monstrous.'
'What they've done is magnificent.'
'Will they come back?'
'Yes – and go again and again – till the landing is made, and the moon is conquered. This is only a beginning . . . for man, no rest and no ending. He must go on, conquest beyond conquest. First this little planet and its winds and waves, and then all the laws of mind and matter that restrain him. Then the planets about him and, at last, out across immensity to the stars.
And when he has conquered all the deeps of space and time, still he will be beginning . . .'

(Alexander Korda, *Things to Come*, 1936)

Even if the individual dies, the race goes on. This is the conclusion to Alexander Korda's film version of *Things to Come* (1936), based on H. G. Wells' *The Shape of Things to Come* (1933). Disaster may strike, but the human race will progress. In its own day, this film did not prosper particularly but it is one of the great classics of sf cinema, self-confidently embodying 'the myth of space flight as the beginning of humankind's transcendence'.[19]

The story runs through a disastrous world war, the recovery of civilizations under the leadership of technocrats, and then the struggle to send people into space against the opposition of effete artists. It closes rhapsodically with the fathers of the pioneers staring out through a great lens into space. Raymond Massey, his eyes lit fanatically, pronounces his verdict on humanity's destiny, to go on, to conquer the planets and then move on to other planets and then to the stars, so there will be no death and no end:'It is this or that, all the universe or nothingness. Which shall it be?'

The film ends with a heavenly chorus intoning the question. Science itself has become a religion.

Chapter 7

Science and religion
Part two: eggheads and energy

Sit, Jessica: look, how the floor of heaven
Is thick inlaid with patines of bright gold:
There's not the smallest orb which thou behold'st
But in his motion like an angel sings,
Still quiring to the young-eyed cherubins;
Such harmony is in immortal souls;
But, whilst this muddy vesture of decay
Doth grossly close it in, we cannot hear it.

(Shakespeare, *The Merchant of Venice*, V. 1)[1]

Gnosticism

If it is true that science fiction is indeed a religion it would
explain some of the hostility science fiction often exercises
towards religion – as a fellow competitor in the same market.
Sf writers themselves acknowledge 'how often sf reads like
religion-for-unbelievers'.[2] With its own priests (scientists),
prophets (sf writers) and true believers (fandom) its faith is
that of the triumphant rise of science, leaving superstition
trampled in its wake. I would argue that there is an inherent
connection between sf and myth, that sf is often a form of
'scientific Gnosticism'.

As Peter Brown points out, the idea that the soul was
associated with the timeless and inviolable realm of 'the
heavens' persisted as far down as Shakespeare. It is elo-
quently expressed in Portia's speech quoted above. The view
of the body presented here ('this muddy vesture of decay') is

clearly not an affirmative one; it 'doth grossly close . . . in' and prevent our hearing of the celestial music. By contrast, to truly behold the heavens is to be reminded that we truly exist as immortal (disembodied) souls, and are inherently linked with divinity.

Gnosticism was a disparate movement in the Ancient Mediterranean world, born of Greek culture and thriving particularly between about 70 and 250 AD (after which it was followed by an even more gloomy successor, Manicheism, a blend of Gnosticism and Zoroastrianism). It was one of the oldest and most potent Christian heresies. Gnosticism is notable for an emphasis on two aspects: dualism and gnosis.[3]

Dualism is the belief that the universe is divided into two parts, one superior and good and the other inferior or actually bad. A rigid form of dualism would regard the soul/mind/spirit to be in the first category, the body/matter/flesh to be in the second. Similarly split are eternity and time, changelessness and transience, the universal and the particular, the idea and the concrete phenomenon. Salvation is to be found by an escape for the soul from the prison of the body. The aim is to leave transience behind and establish a firm grip on an unalterable reality.

The second aspect of Gnosticism was the emphasis on remembering. Gnosticism itself is named after the Greek word for knowledge, *gnosis*. Gnosticism was the way of salvation in which the initiate was lifted from the world of the senses to the world of eternal unchanging ideas by the impartation of secret knowledge. The secret was one's own fundamental identity with the divine, that one's essential identity was as a disembodied 'divine spark'. However, separated from the root of being by the descent of the soul into the body and preyed upon by the deceits of evil, one forgot the truth and needed to be reminded of it. 'Remember who you are!' was the watchword. In some forms of Gnosticism, a heavenly redeemer brought the sacred knowledge of salvation, of the illusion of evil and the body. It naturally followed that to be saved was to be liberated from the lowly body.

Despite the peculiarities of its mythology, Gnosticism has much in common with science fiction. Sf, although seemingly born of the materialism of science with its worldly concentration, often strives to leave the body and the physical realm behind, precisely matching Gnosticism's emphasis on the unreality of the physical world as opposed to the 'real' immaterial one.[4]

In addition, science fiction – like Gnosticism – believes in the fundamental virtue of knowledge. As in much ancient Greek thinking, sin was not so much a matter of a moral failure of the will as of a sheer lack of information. The belief that the basic problem is ignorance was shared by the Enlightenment. Education, the giving of knowledge would solve everything. In Gnosticism, all the problems of living are the result of not knowing the secret of existence; in sf, knowledge is similarly exalted. The modernist age is about knowledge and the use of it, raising issue of power and control; the difficult ethical questions tend not to be addressed. In other words, 'What?' and 'How?', not 'Why?' and 'Whether?' Sf tends to exalt in sheer amounts of information. This is why the 'power' of modern computers has found a rather adulatory audience in sf fans.

Extra-sensory perception

'Listen,' he cried in exaltation. 'Listen, Normals! You must learn what it is. You must learn how it is. You must tear the barriers down. You must tear the veils away. We see the truth you cannot see. That there is nothing in man but love and faith, courage and kindness, generosity and sacrifice. All else is only the barrier of your blindness. One day we'll all be mind to mind and heart to heart. . . .'

(Alfred Bester, *The Demolished Man*)[5]

One of the dreams of sf is to overcome the boundaries of human being. Telepathy above all offers a tempting shortcut. The difficulties we have in understanding one another are only physical: if we could only speak openly mind to mind, they would vanish. A golden age would arrive. Alfred Bester's novels *Tiger! Tiger!* (1956) and *The Demolished Man* (1953) offer a vision of a new dynamic history for humankind.

The belief that human life had to escape the exigencies of

bodily existence expressed itself particularly in the 1950s in tales of esp (extra-sensory perception). Enthusiastic readers were reminded of the limitations of their bodily existence. They had to have mental powers that enabled those physical limits to be broken: to be able to tell the future (precognition), read other people's minds (telepathy), move objects by the power of the mind alone (telekinesis) and so on. It is perhaps not surprising that L. Ron Hubbard, then practising as sf writer René Lafayette, found a welcome in the sf field for first Dianetics, then Scientology itself as he developed it 'both as technique and as religion'. The essence of Hubbard's idea was 'a technology of self-improvement, a set of instructions to follow in order to liberate the transcendent power within one'.[6]

Story after story told of the super-child with unknown powers, waiting to be let loose on an unsuspecting world which would seek to destroy it if it knew the truth. Typical works were Henry Kuttner's *Baldy* series (1943–53), Wilson Tucker's *Wild Talent* (1954) and John Wyndham's *The Chrysalids* (1955). The figure of the boy Jonny Cross in A. E. Van Vogt's *Slan* (1940; book 1946) is in many ways emblematic of this genre – the superboy, discovering his powers, learning how to use them to advantage.

In Frederick Pohl's 'The Gold at the Starbow's End' (1972), the 'evolution to godhood' element of the theme becomes clear. Here a scientific experiment sees a spaceship dispatched to Alpha Centauri on a ten-year trip, deliberately designed to go wrong and thus give its crew ten years alone 'to think'. This they proceed to do, developing into superhuman beings and creating a world around Alpha Centauri because there is not one there already. Angry at the deceit, they return in a chilling conclusion to take revenge on their experimenters: 'great golden ships from Alpha-Aleph landed and disgorged their bright, terrible crewmen to clean up the Earth'.[7]   As with much sf, the assumption is that their mental superiority justifies their actions.

The desire for a clear cut apocalypse, a sorting out of sheep from goats, is to be found in much science fiction. The ruthlessness displayed to enemies of the messianic solution is scary. In Robert Silverberg's *Master of Life and Death* (1957), an all-powerful human despot controls overpopulation with a dictatorial hand. Poul Anderson's 'The Burning Bridge' (1960) concerns a first human interstellar journey: when a crewman hears from the communications operator of a recall message he has just received from Earth he kills him and destroys the message. Nothing must come between humanity and its destiny.

No matter? Never mind!

> Flesh couldn't grasp the realities of mind and spirit that were liberated from flesh. Babies! A home! And the whole grubby animal-business of eating and drinking and sleeping! How could anyone ask him to stay in the mire when the stars challenged over-head? He walked slowly down the street, alone in the night, an apprentice godling renouncing mortality.
>
> (Frederick Pohl and Cyril Kornbluth, Wolfbane)[8]

In Frederick Pohl and Cyril Kornbluth's *Wolfbane* (1959) the message yet again is of the inconsequentiality of matter. The hero – in destroying alien machines – becomes part of a 'snowflake', a telepathically linked entity of eight individuals. This escape from the body is seen as liberation from 'the mire', 'flesh . . . babies . . . home . . . the whole grubby animal-business of eating and drinking and sleeping'.

Many other works have the same theme, that is, that 'mankind's aspirations go beyond the grossly fleshly condition'.[9] Damon Knight's 'Four in One' (1953) tells of explorers on an alien planet being absorbed into a mindless protoplasm which dissolves their bodies but not their brains. Far from being regarded as a disaster, this is considered a good thing. The hero, his essence now part of the new creature, entitles it, '*Spes hominis*: Man's hope'. Douglas Robillard writes, 'there seems to be a feeling, expressed or acquiesced in silently, that mankind, as a kind, is far from the perfection of creation. Another step is needed to ensure its advancement and, at times, even its survival. . . . There is no regret in the loss of the human, and the turn to the inhuman is accepted eagerly.'

Science fiction has always believed in the 'plasticity' of humanity. It evolves and changes naturally and artificially. Transformation to a different mode of being occurs in Clifford Simak's 'Desertion' (1944) and Robert Silverberg's *Downward to the Earth* (1969), where humans are genetically engineered for adaption to a hostile environment. In Frederick Pohl's *Man Plus* (1976) 'poor Roger Torraway' has his genitals removed after he is forced to volunteer for a Mars-colonization project: however, he gains solar-panel wings.[10] What is significant in almost all these stories is the assumption that since the essence of the person is the mind or soul, what happens to the body is, as it were (pardon the pun), immaterial.

The first stage in this process is to identify the self with the brain. Thus in the singularly entertaining 'Spock's Brain' episode of *Star Trek*, the object of the title is 'brainnapped' and used to run a vast underground computer. Kirk and McCoy set out in search of it, manipulating Spock's mechanically ambulating body by means of a box with switches till they can find and reattach its brain in an even more hilarious scene.

The next stage, but one that is strangely more readily accepted, is the idea that our true identity is independent of all matter, even the brain. Thus in the notoriously sexist 'Turnabout Intruder', a vindictive Dr Janice Lester swaps identities with James Kirk, who finds himself struggling for recognition in a woman's body. There is some awareness that we are, at least, partly corporeal by the fact that everyone has to be 'put back together again right' in the end. In all these stories, the fundamental idea, however, is thoroughly Cartesian: I am fundamentally identical with my mind/ brain, and having a body (or even the 'wrong' body) is irrel- evant to this. Thus in one classic *Dr Who* story ('The Three Doctors') a rogue Time Lord caught in a black hole was actually reduced by radiation to incorporeality. Nevertheless, he still existed, as 'pure will'.

This notion of the abandonment of the body is elsewhere often seen as beneficial. Greg Bear's *Anvil of Stars* (1992) tells us that 'many civilisations reduce their presence to information matrices, abandoning their physical forms, and living as pure mentality'.[11] The most poetic – and influential

– rendition of the dualist theme is probably Clarke's *2001: A Space Odyssey*, where the main character is transformed by aliens at the end of the tale into a wondrous, glowing 'Star-Child'.[12] This is seen, as often elsewhere in sf, as the culmination of development – a leaving of the body behind, and a progression to 'a higher level of existence'.

One word has been repeatedly used above: 'pure'. 'Pure will', 'pure mentality', 'pure energy'. Why are these things supposed to be pure? By contrast, what is considered to be 'impure'? Obviously, the answer is matter, the body, physicality. According to Einsteinian relativity (the famous $e = mc^2$) energy and matter are equivalent. Yet, somehow, a science fiction that supposedly not only dwells in the latter part of the twentieth century but is also able to anticipate the future, operates with a thoroughly dualistic notion of energy being 'pure' as opposed, presumably, to thoroughly 'impure' matter. Once again, this is scarcely a positive view of creation.

Unease

Sf is, however, nothing if not varied and, therefore, responses to this dualist vision are not always so enthusiastic. None of the dissenting opinions, for all this, deny the possibility of such transformations – just their advisability. John Wyndham's speculations about superhumans find their negative side, for example, in *The Midwich Cuckoos* (1957), filmed as *Village of the Damned* (1960) with its chilling alien-impregnated children. The Martians of H. G. Wells' *The War of the Worlds* are also distinctly unpleasant: cold and heartless. Terry Nation's Daleks, which terrified a generation of children when first brought to the TV screen in BBC's *Dr Who* in 1963 (for all the creatures' legendary inability to climb steps!), are in the same vein. They express what Colin Manlove describes as the essential dualism of much science fiction: mind and matter, humanity and environment.[13]

It is not by accident that the Daleks live in a city surrounded by a world ruined by nuclear war. On the planet Skaro mind literally has destroyed matter. The Daleks themselves are the remnants of a humanoid race who, having brought devastation upon themselves and their world, now live as mutated monsters imprisoned in mechanical shells. Lingering radiation and loathsome beasts dominate the exterior world, together with survivors more human in appearance (the Thals) who have disavowed violence because of the war. *Dr Who*'s Cybermen and *Star Trek*'s Borg are similar in nature: humanoids who have gradually replaced their organic parts with electronics have become ruthless emotionless cybernetic killing machines.

The film *Forbidden Planet* (1954) gave a parallel message. It is a surprisingly mature work based on Shakespeare's *The Tempest*. It begins with a military expedition finding the survivors of a colonizing ship on Rigel IV. Welcomed, though unenthusiastically, by Dr Morbius, the visitors are told that all apart from he and his daughter were inexplicably destroyed years before by some irresistible, though apparently immaterial, monster. Soon the new arrivals too are prey to attacks. Eventually it is revealed that the attacker is, in fact, Dr Morbius himself – or, rather, a 'monster from the Id', conjured up unknowingly from his subconscious mind. It can do this because it can tap the enormous energy plants created by the planet's previous inhabitants, the Krell. They, it turns out, were themselves destroyed by their own subconscious minds 'in one night' millions of years previously as they sought to become creatures 'of pure mind, without physical instrumentality'.

Here there is a real warning about the quest for 'pure creation', and the dangers of arrogance. There is a more mature recognition that becoming 'pure mind' might be a rather mixed blessing. For the rest of us, the yelling of children repeating in supposedly remorseless Dalek tones of increasing hysteria, 'Exterminate! Exterminate!' is enough to give us pause!

The identification of mind and soul

Only one thing in the universe grows fuller, and richer, and forces its way uphill. Intelligence – human lives – we're the only things there are that don't obey the universal law. The universe kills our bodies . . . in the end,

it kills our brains. But our minds . . . . There's the precious
thing; there's the phenomenon that has nothing to do
with time and space except to use them . . .

(Algis Budrys, *Rogue Moon*)[14]

That mind is primary in sf is shown in many stories. In A.
E. Van Vogt's priceless story, 'The Proxy Intelligence', an
alien is invulnerable simply because 'above a certain level of
I.Q. mind actually is over matter. A being above that intelligence level cannot be killed. Not by bullet, nor by any cir-
cumstance involving matter.'[15] In sf's very intellectualism
and its propensity for 'the idea as hero', the human mind is
kept at the forefront. Clarke, Heinlein, Knight and Simak
at the most basic level incline to Gnosticism through their
allegiance to the idea that the most important reality is
mental. Philip José Farmer, A. E. Van Vogt, Frederick Pohl
and Cyril Kornbluth, Greg Bear go even further in this
direction. The identification of the mind with the deepest
aspect of human essence leads on easily to an association (as
in Descartes) between the mind and the soul.

In no author is this so obvious as Julian May, whose best-
selling fantasy/sf works are sustained by the evolutionary
speculations of twentieth-century Roman Catholic anthropologist and priest Pierre Teilhard de Chardin.[16] De Chardin's
thought is recruited by May to support her narrative edifice
of the development of psi powers among humans. The
arbiters of the Galactic Milieu act under the advice of Lylmik
Overseers – disembodied entities of pure mind (surprise,
surprise). Of these, the most important is 'Atoning Unifex',
a six-million year old man who, when Marc Remillard,
caused a galactic war that killed millions through his
attempts to create 'Mental Man'. Though premature, this
was considered a step in the right direction. The aim is to
develop a new, psychically-gifted human race.

This idealization of 'mentality' is continued in the presen-
tation of 'Saint Jack the Bodiless', one of these beings who
abandons his decaying body to maintain existence as a
noncorporeal being. He occasionally 'wears' a body of his own
construction so as to help others' scruples. There is plenty of
mention of prayer in this saga, but none of Christ, for all that

de Chardin saw him as representing the Omega Point, the ultimate end of evolution.

Is mentality, though, the same as wisdom? Is sheer weight of knowledge as important as love? Sf here (as in Iain M. Banks' *Feersum Endjinn*, 1994 and Vernor Vinge's *A Fire upon the Deep*, 1992) crudely equates information with God. This is banal, inexcusable even in an age which worships computers!

Of all religious gurus, de Chardin's ideas are most susceptible for use by sf. They are central too to the *Hyperion* (1989–) saga of Dan Simmons. In this vast epic (continued in *Endymion*, 1996) future history is the backcloth for a titanic apocalyptic battle between 'the human UI' ('Ultimate Intelligence', i.e., God) and the 'computer UI' (a construction of 'AIs' – Artificial Intelligences). In most modern sf – as John Clute has observed[17] – AIs are how sf writers think of God: immaterial, vastly powerful, omniscient, uncaring.

It could be argued that de Chardin is so popular in sf because he represents its own view of 'naturalistic vitalism': as he says himself, 'all that exists is matter becoming spirit'.[18] According to this view, the universe is evolving into God, a God who, increasingly in the modern world view, is seen as 'the vital force of the universe struggling to realise itself'.[19] Gnosticism appears once again in the repudiation of matter and the identification of spirit with mind.

Some Gnostic sf writers

The mid twentieth-century British writer Olaf Stapledon gave to sf a vast cosmic 'spiritual' perspective in which the evolution of humanity is located. He has himself been placed alongside H. G. Wells as one of the giants of the genre, for all that he may be 'more revered than read'. His *Star Maker* (1937) has been described as 'the one great grey holy book of science fiction'.[20] His 'chill but intoxicating vision'[21] won its most significant disciple in Arthur C. Clarke, who has himself joined the normally accepted pantheon of sf writers and is increasingly regarded as a media guru. Stapledon's *Last and First Men* (1930) encompasses nothing less than the whole of human history, past and future. Of this novel, Brian

Aldiss writes: 'Man is the hero of the chronicle; men are of little account. Of the 200 million members of the human race, the narrative tells us laconically at one point "All were burnt or roasted or suffocated within three months – all but 35, who happened to be in the neighbourhood of the North Pole".'[22]

Aldiss sees all Stapledon's works as engaged 'in putting homo sapiens in his proper perspective'.[23] To this end the transience of humanity's attachment to its own planet is emphasized: 'man's sojourn on Venus lasted somewhat longer than his whole career on Earth'.[24] Humanity, which has previously been assaulted by Martians and almost wiped out, eventually migrates again to Neptune. In all, it progresses through eighteen different kinds of 'Men', and the story is supposedly told by a message sent back through history from the last of the eighteenth Men, two billion years in the future. In the meantime, Men have adapted to the water and the air, and been genetically altered several times.

The cosmic vision is aided by a number of temporal charts purporting to show human history which grow ever larger in scope as the book proceeds: the pretension is entirely characteristic of sf. The purpose of the whole narrative is the same: 'the sense that we are as sparrows that fall – and without any divine glance cast in our direction as we go'.[25] It is about 'the combined greatness and insignificance of man'. The conclusion is that 'it is very good to have been man'. Humanity indeed is the tale's tragic hero.

Star Maker expands to an even greater level of magnitude – the history of the universe, stretching over a hundred billion years. Such a novel can never be outdone. The story begins with the author leaving behind his 'atom of community' as a result of a domestic argument to stand alone on a hill at night underneath the stars; from there he is lifted up mentally to nearby stars to discover the peculiarities of a world similar to ours, 'the other Earth', whose inhabitants fight over issues of the sense, taste. His knowledge and sympathies are extended as he journeys on with a representative of that world to increasingly alien worlds and beings ('ichthyoids', 'arachnoids'); then on to increasingly larger collections of beings – world-minds, system-minds, sub-galactic minds, symbiotic worlds and living stars, galactic minds, the Cosmic Mind and, finally, the evolving 'Star Maker' itself, a being beyond good and evil, who contemplates eternally not just this universe but the infinity of possible universes.

Star Maker is described by Robert Scholes and Eric Rabkin as 'the most serious work of science fiction'.[26] Its scope is colossal; it deliberately uses scale to awe; its invention is prodigious, its ambition huge. This is a vision of the universe characterized by 'dispassionate objectivity'.[27] Stapledon's talk about community (as witnessed by the increasing aggregation of individual sentients into collectives) resolves into the ultimate importance of knowledge, the impersonal accumulation of 'how things are', the cold pitiless gaze of the 'Star Maker' itself.

Arthur C. Clarke expresses a similar vision repeatedly. The universe is beyond our grasp (even if it will eventually wear out) and we are dwarfed by it. This is simultaneously our tragedy and glory – to live in this universe and to grasp it conceptually is to celebrate 'the brief music that is man'.[28]

In his writings (for example, his correspondence with H. G. Wells) Stapledon shows an incredible animosity to Christianity; but it is as a rival.[29] As Aldiss says, '*Last and First Men* is just slightly an atheist's tract . . . . In *Star Maker*, the atheism has become a faith in itself'.[30] Whilst Stapledon adores the 'human spirit', he shows no real compassion for individuals. It is 'Man' who counts.

This 'spiritual' vision claims to provide a viewpoint that relativizes our normal concentration on the business of living, and to elevate our minds above that. It operates in almost Hegelian dialectical fashion between 'the atom of community' and 'the cold light of the stars'. The appeal of science fiction is partially because of this Marxist-style objectivism – the appeal of regarding humanity from the summit of Mount Olympus and looking like a god with the eyes of eternity down at the petty squabbles of antlike humans far below. It is hardly surprising that in *Odd John* (1935) Stapledon's evolutionary supermen do not hesitate to murder and engage in gruesome genetic experiments with human subjects when it is convenient for them to do so. Stapledon, in the person of the narrator, rebukes himself for his feelings of repugnance at these acts. It seems quite clear that C. S. Lewis' *That Hideous Strength* (1945) – in which ruthless scientists in league with the Devil engage in vivisection and murder – had Stapledon in mind. Stapledon himself had no doubt: he wrote for the 'wideawakes' – rather like L. Ron Hubbard in his *Mission Earth* series.[31]

David Lindsay's *A Voyage to Arcturus* (1920) – a work that also much affected C. S. Lewis – goes even further in certain respects. It is positively Manichaean in its depreciation of this world. Illusion dominates. Good and evil turn out (rather as in Mozart's *Magic Flute*) to be very different to what is expected. Sensuous enjoyment of pleasure masquerades as good but is actually evil, and perpetually feeds off the real good as a parasite. Creation, the physical, the body is deception, dragging the soul down into its clutches. Only pain and suffering offer escape. As in the Gnostic doctrine of the demiurge (which is also hinted at in Stapledon), creation is the morass from which we need to be rescued.

Sf and Gnosticism

As Robert Galbreath comments, the fact that not all sf goes so far as these last examples is not in itself terribly significant: 'I am not claiming that such literature necessarily adheres to Gnosticism as a worldview, or even that it employs Gnostic themes and structures' (for all the examples which in fact do exist to support this viewpoint). . . . 'My point rather is that [it] exemplifies a modern version of Gnosis as revelatory saving knowledge of the transcendental.' In terms of this definition, the hero of Heinlein's 'Universe' who sees the stars for the first time is given saving knowledge – even if many others refuse to be saved.[32] 'From the perspective of the characters within fantastic narratives, the knowledge they obtain often does alter them, sometimes profoundly. In any fantastic texts, this knowledge enables characters literally to save themselves, their souls, their world, or humanity.' This may be at the level of *Dr Who*; it may be in the ideative mazes of Isaac Asimov and Frank Herbert; it may be in the perhaps unconsciously Gnostic speculations of Bob Shaw[33] or the consciously Gnostic ones of Philip K. Dick's *The Three*

Stigmata of Palmer Eldritch (1965), *Ubik* (1969) and *The Divine Invasion* (1981).

In Dick's *Valis* (1981) it is revelations in shafts of pink light from the orbiting VALIS satellite that provides the information that reveals the truth about history. (We learn that Richard Nixon is the Antichrist, for example; perhaps not much of a surprise for Dick's left-wing hippy friends.) VALIS stands for 'Vast Active Living Intelligent System' – that is to say, God. Dick conflates together artificial intelligence, apostolic Christianity, the Gnosticism of Nag Hammadi, Siddharta, Dionysus and Apollo, Ikhnaton and Psalm 104, as well as the fish sign of the apostolic Christians and the Double Helix. Simultaneously, he expresses this in the street language of contemporary California, thus rooting all the weirdness in a peculiar down to earth situation.

Valis concludes with the announcement by the two year old child, Sophia (incarnation of wisdom) that human beings should give up worshipping all deities other than itself. This revelation – that humanity is itself God – is the central message of the book, the secret which makes its followers the elect possessors of the truth. Whilst sf critics argue whether *Valis* is sf or not, it can be argued to be so on the basis of this message.[34] The fundamental immanentist strain in this thinking is also to be seen in *Star Wars*' concept of 'the Force'. As Douglas Mackey points out, the Gnostic knows that ultimately creation (or at least part of it) and God are at root identical.[35] Gnosticism abolishes the distinction between the Creator and creature which the Judaic religions (Judaism, Christianity, Islam) all hold. Sf too, without the Judaeo-Christian God, tends to make humanity itself divine. It inaugurates the millennium. It is the language of the New Age.[36]

Chapter 8

The divinity of creation

There is something about seeing a launch – the electric excitement of it, the overpowering grandeur of a giant rocket climbing into the sky slowly, inexorably, driven on by billowing tongues of flame – that's the closest thing to a religious experience that many of us have ever had.

Hardened sceptics break into tears, when you see a 50-story tall column of intricate machinery detach itself from this planet and carry not only a few astronauts but also all the hopes and fears of the human race outward toward the infinite universe, you can never view your own life, the world, or the space program in the same old way again.

(Ben Bova)[1]

What we have dealt with thus far are the spiritual dreams of science fiction. What becomes interesting from a theological point of view is not just that humanity is striving to fill the gap vacated by the absence of God ('a humanity of the gaps' rather than 'God of the gaps', as it were), but that the way in which humanity seeks to define itself is in terms of the manner God has traditionally been defined. It is striking that, in the portrayal of humanity, aliens and the universe, sf passes the supposed traditional attributes of God on to these aspects of creation: omnipresence, omniscience, omnipotence, infinity, invisibility, incorporeality, ineffability, immortality, impassibility. Could it be that humanity has no more got this right than in its rejection of God's existence altogether – that is, it understands no more *who* he is than *whether* he is? Gene Roddenberry was always railing at 'god' figures in *Star Trek*:[2] had he missed the entire point?

To infinity and beyond

We have already examined the extent to which sf is the religion of space. For sf, space means, among other things, boundlessness (the literal meaning of 'infinity').

In the late 1960s and early 1970s, the 'space music' used by the BBC to announce its coverage of launches from Cape Canaveral was the dramatic opening chords from Richard Strauss' *Also Sprach Zarathustra* (also used by Stanley Kubrick for his paeon to space travel, the film *2001: A Space Odyssey*). This is ironic as Strauss' literary original was philosopher Friedrich Nietzsche's *Also Sprach Zarathustra* (1883–92) ('Thus Spake Zarathustra') – a hymn to heroic nihilism! God is dead, he declared, and we can be supermen. Let us throw off the past and dare to realize ourselves.

Nietzsche himself came into disrepute through association with Nazi ideology; not surprisingly as his call to abandon the slave-religion of Christianity with its enervating concentration on the cross, the weak and lowly chimed in with Hitler's thinking. The emphasis on the race as the collective *Übermensch* (Superman) rings chillingly close to the human 'racism' we often find in science fiction.

The linking of destiny and space is common. James Michener has written of the space programme as an expression of America's 'Manifest Destiny', extending the New Frontier of John F. Kennedy beyond the borders of the planet into the universe at large.[3] In the nineteenth century such belief had not only allowed, but indeed commanded, expansion into the hinterland of the USA – and too bad for anyone who happened to be there first. In Australia, indeed, the continent was described as *terra nullius*, 'uninhabited'; the Aborigines, then, obviously *should* not be there and could be cheerfully disposed of. As has been pointed out, Arthur C. Clarke's view of the Renaissance voyages of discovery as part of a movement towards human maturation unfortunately ignores the impact of these journeys on the natives of those lands unfortunate enough to be thus 'discovered' – the Americas, 'the brave new world' of Columbus, Cortez and Pizarro, being the outstanding example.[4]

This notion of the world as the white man's plaything has

persisted till remarkably recently. Similarly humanity expands into 'space' to fulfil its destiny. Conceptually, the last few centuries in the West have seen the rise of the human subject, considered both individually ('the artist as Romantic hero') and collectively ('the race'). Our age has been simultaneously one of extreme individualism (the USA, perhaps above all) and collectivism (Nazism and Communism). Feeding off one another, and sometimes seesawing apocalyptically one way and then the other within one country and society (as in France since the French Revolution of 1789), they represent not opposites but opposite poles of the same dilemma – the self-assertion of the human subject. Such self-assertion needs an object to fight against – God, aliens, any 'other' that stands in its way and threatens to limit it.

The notion of expansion into space is often symbolized by the planet Mars. There has recently been an extraordinary number of novels about the colonization of Mars.[5] The furore has been encouraged by the speculations about Martian life supposedly revealed by the famous Antarctic meterorite (ALH 84001).[6] A discussion in current leading sf magazine, *Sf Age* took an enthusiastic line about colonization. 'Mars is the next step to ensure the survival of humankind, expand off this fragile planet and on to the stars.' 'We should go to Mars to explore, to find out about the place of life in the universe, and to begin the process of spreading life throughout the universe – our kind of life, that is' (!) 'The urge to explore space is the most noble and selfless dream of humankind. If we do not go forward, to Mars and beyond, we will inevitably slide backward and be forgotten by history. H. G. Wells said it all: in the end it will either be the stars or nothing at all.'[7]

In mainstream sf, particularly that published in John Campbell's 1950s *Astounding Science Fiction*, humanity was normally able to overcome any attempt to restrict it to its own planet or conquer it – simply by virtue of its quick-wittedness and technological precocity.[8] Eric Frank Russell's work in particular frequently took the form of bungling aliens being thwarted by ingenious humans. 'Often one man was sufficient to tackle an entire species'.[9] This sub-genre was extremely popular. Poul Anderson's *The High Crusade*

(1960) is typical in telling 'a delightful wish-fulfilment conception' of a medieval baron and his entourage conquering an alien interstellar empire.[10] In David Brin's popular *Startide Rising* (1983), 'wolfling' humans similarly defy their galactic overlords. The clear message is that a precocious humanity is intended to rule the universe – as Kipling's white sahib the Raj and Pizarro the Incas. Exploration of, and dominance of, the galaxy, in material or spiritual form, is generally regarded in sf as essential for any decent, self-respecting human race.

Humanity on trial

Humanity's right to defy all boundaries and break all limits is enthusiastically endorsed by most sf. Weston in C. S. Lewis' satirical *Out of the Silent Planet* (1938) represents its most extreme expression. He justifies his colonialist actions before his accusers by claiming humanity's inalienable right to go where it wishes and do what it wishes.[11] This is what civilization means. For Lewis, space travel is all too likely to be a way in which we spread our own kind of disease throughout a universe that could well do without it. 'We know what our race does to strangers. Man destroys or enslaves every species he can. Civilised man murders, enslaves, cheats and corrupts savage man.'[12] Before the ruler of Mars humanity is judged and found wanting – and restricted to its own planet.

We may contrast Lewis' story with Robert Heinlein's juvenile novel, *Have Spacesuit, Will Travel* (1958). In this tale, two human children similarly end up at the bar of a galactic court, defending the human race against accusations of human brutality and violence. The boy is as defiant as Weston. 'We have no limits! There's no telling what our future will be.'[13] 'We'll make a star or die trying.'[14] Unlike Lewis, however, Heinlein salutes this. Wollheim writes: 'in their own way so say Simak and Chandler and Smith and Anderson and a myriad others who fill the pages of the *real* science fiction magazines and the *real* science fiction books that crowd the newsstands and bookstores of the world'.[15] In Lewis' story the self-consciously noble protagonist for this point of view is both pompous and ridiculous; here he is heroic.

Ultimately this is identical to the gung-ho response of *Independence Day* – expressed towards anyone who gets in the way of human self-expression. Like Hitler's *Volk*, the human race demands *Lebensraum* (territory for expansion) in order to fulfil its spiritual destiny.

Immortality Inc.

We shall cover some of the other classical attributes of God in more depth in subsequent chapters. Incorporeality we have already dealt with in the desire in sf to pass beyond bodilyness, matter, flesh and blood for an existence as 'pure energy', 'pure mentality'. Humanity's journey into space is about both infinity and omnipresence. It is to immortality that we now turn our attention. Donald Wollheim thus sums up his own faith:

> Whatever may be, I am sure of one thing. There is a famous poem which has the constant refrain, 'This is the way the world ends.
>
>> Well . . . .
>> We are not going to end with a bang.
>> We are not going to end with a whisper.
>> We are not going to end.
>> That's all.[16]

For Wollheim, Arthur C. Clarke's novel *Against the Fall of Night* (1956) is to be applauded for its 'faith in man's immortality'.[17] The fact that '. . . in this last city . . . the last act is to send a message out into the universe where somewhere there must still be men to carry the word that Mankind would come back' tells him that this is 'a beautiful book, an act of faith for a science-fiction mind'.

Immortality does not just belong to sf for all that it is described by Stephen Clark as maybe its only theme.[18] It is an age-old dream. It is to be found in the angelic elves of J. R. R. Tolkein's *The Lord of the Rings*, in the figures of ageless

Ransom and Merlin of C. S. Lewis' *That Hideous Strength* and in the figure of deathless Ayesha in Rider Haggard's *She* (1887). In all of these, though, it either tends to backfire or have its own disadvantages – like an eternity of pain and sorrow! Yet sf presents it in many ways – as the result of cryogenic freezing, rejuvenation potions and diets, selective breeding, genetic engineering, nanotechnological self-repair or 'uploading' onto computers.[19] In Kim Stanley Robinson's *Red Mars* (1992) scientists find a way to eliminate the errors caused in information transfer between cells. Whether bestowed by an immortal flame (as in *She*) or by means of an atomic explosion (Fredric Brown's 'Letter to a Phoenix', 1954), the same aim is in view – the hope of liberation from the most terrifying limitation of all, death. We cannot be divine if we actually die! The immortality of the human species may be of some consolation for our own individual deaths. For Brown, humanity itself (the 'Phoenix' of the title) is the only immortal organism in the universe. It is interesting that this story is frequently noted in sf circles as philosophically satisfying.[20]

The limitlessness of sheer size is respected in sf and is often seen as akin to immortality. The 'big dumb object' (BDO) – a human or alien cultural artefact that outwaits the ages – is often used to evoke awe. This is true of the vast, never fully explored or grasped interstellar craft of Arthur C. Clarke's *Rendezvous with Rama* (1973), the colossal million-Earth area of Larry Niven's *Ringworld* (1970) and the Dyson sphere of Bob Shaw's *Orbitsville* (1975).[21]

James Blish's *Cities in Flight* (1950–62) depicted a double solution to the normal constraints of nature: the discovery of antigravity 'spindizzies' that enable cities literally (and metaphorically?) to unroot themselves from the earth and travel through the galaxy; and also antiagathic drugs which postpone death for ever for the few lucky enough to have access to them.[22] It is perhaps not surprising that the last book in the series has Mayor Amalfi of New York as the creator of a new universe as this one comes to an end.

Similarly in Poul Anderson's *Tau Zero* (1967) the end of the universe is outlived. When the spacecraft *Lenore Christian* is damaged, she cannot decelerate. Irresistibly gathering speed from the interstellar dust she uses to power her engines, she travels ever more rapidly between the stars, then through our own galaxy till eventually she is racing through entire other galaxies in a matter of seconds. Since vast amounts of 'objective' time are passing, ultimately she outlives the whole universe. Apart from the generally acknowledged ludicrousness of this conclusion (for she could not be 'outside' what happens), the astonishing thing about this story is that it is otherwise entirely feasible according to our present understanding of physics. This sheer extraordinariness of reality is here what evokes awe.

An eternal universe?

Stanley Jaki has commented on the frequent affection among scientists for the idea of an unending universe, that even if humanity dies out, the universe itself does not:[23] there is something comforting in that! As the subtitle of one of his works suggests (*From Eternal Cycles to an Oscillating Universe*),[24] Jaki sees the current popularity of the 'oscillating universe' as being in continuity with the ancient Greek belief in an eternal universe. According to this, the universe's expansion from a 'Big Bang' will turn into retraction into a 'Big Crunch', from which there will be another expansion as a result of a 'Big Bounce' – and so on forever. Cosmologist Steven Weinberg openly admits that his preference for the 'oscillating universe' hypothesis is based on philosophical preferences: he simply does not like the idea of a beginning.[25] For Jaki, this is precisely the point. To give immortality to the universe gives it also a measure of divinity.

This emphasis on an eternity of repetition leads science fiction naturally towards myth because of the latter's emphasis on the recurrent cyclical patterns typical of both Eastern and ancient Greek thinking.[26] By contrast, the modern concept of history is based on the supposition of linear development, something that, it has been argued, is also the legacy of a Judaeo-Christian outlook. Proponents of an eternal universe prefer the mythic model of the repeated rise-and-fall of civilizations. 'The myth of progress' and 'the myth of eternal cycles' are both typical of science fiction, and are often wedded together as in Olaf Stapledon's *Last and First Men*. Greg Bear's *Eon* (1985) and *Eternity* (1988) feature another BDO but one that literally opens on infinity; they are in the same vein.

Casey Fredericks' *The Future of Eternity* (1982) emphasizes the link between science fiction and mythical cyclicality, pointing out the significance in sf of 'the big time', sheer size. Immensity is supposed to be a pointer to significance – and the universe is full of that! The underlying assumption tends to be that such a big thing surely has to go on forever. Cycles are one of the ways of maintaining a system for eternity. Linearity, then, is only apparent, an illusion; the truth is eternal repetition.

So too sf deals not with individuals, but with 'the fate of the entire world, or some other planet, or the Galactic Empire, or the whole of mankind, or even occasionally the entire universe'.[27]

The very size of the cosmos can both elevate and squash humanity. Stapledon and Clarke want to exalt it but they also can speak of our 'cosmic loneliness', the rarity and vanity of a life in an unfeeling, hostile universe. The size of the universe is an argument used against the so-called human centred outlook of Christianity, but is one that a secular, atheistic approach has to come to terms with also.[28]

Brian Aldiss' *Helliconia* trilogy (1982, 1983, 1985) and *Hothouse* (1962) in their different ways portray humanity as a pawn of nature, whilst simultaneously worshipping the principle of life itself.[29] So too J. G. Ballard's work is a sustained assault on modernism, showing humanity's failure to keep control, for which reason it is castigated by Lem for 'its cognitive pessimism, for its absolute refusal to admit the possibility of change for the better, for its antiscientism'.[30] Yet, as with Aldiss, even in this seeming self-abnegation by humanity in the face of overwhelming nature, it asserts itself against its creaturehood by associating itself with nature and divinizing it.

Aliens

Aliens in science fiction similarly affirm or threaten humanity. Bug-eyed monsters (BEMs) – many-tentacled horrors advancing predaciously on screaming females – dominated early magazine science fiction.[31] By contrast, Steven Spielberg's films portray them as supernaturally attractive – as in *Close Encounters of the Third Kind* (1977), *E.T.* (1982), *Batteries Not Included* (1987) and a host of imitators such as *Starman* (1984) and *Cocoon* (1985). Aliens appearing in welters of kaleidoscopic colours and overwhelming benisons of extraterrestrial love are so nice, it is difficult to understand why we ever worried about them! In these tales, it is the humans who are without exception disbelieving, manipulative, mercenary, militaristic. *E.T.* has as its hero a being from beyond earth who is found in a stable, brings love and liberation but is hounded, dies, rises again and even ascends to heaven. In *Batteries Not Included* tiny flying saucers have the kind of role Frank Capra reserved for Jimmy Stewart's guardian angel in *It's a Wonderful Life* (how much this tells us about the modern age!) *Cocoon* features more life-giving transcendent beings from beyond the stars. 'Heaven' has been repopulated with the mythology of a rational age.[32] Modern science fiction films have produced an overwhelming surge of stories with religious subtexts.

The so-called 'space opera' of early sf almost universally portrayed aliens as rivals for the domination of the universe or even the possession of the Earth. Earth was invaded subtly, even 'in disguise'. 'Taken over' humans could usually be easily identified by their slow mode of speaking, abstracted gaze and small mark on the back of the neck.[33] In E. E. 'Doc' Smith's *Lensman* stories, aliens are divided between exotic human allies on the one hand, and exotic, loathsome fiends who deserve to be – and are – annihilated wholesale and gorily on the other (the Clint Eastwood school of alien relations). In Heinlein's notoriously xenophobic *Starship Troopers* (1959) alien 'Bugs' are blown away as rapidly and destructively as possible. Elsewhere, aliens may act (as in Russell or Anvil) as rather dense and slow-witted foils to a witty, energetic, inventive human race that is obviously on a rapid escalator to the top of whatever hierarchy happens to be around.

Such aliens are not so much alien, that is different, incomprehensible, other, as merely 'different from ourselves', that is, hostile. Indeed, such aliens may be threatening precisely in that similarity. Murray Leinster's story 'First Contact' (1945) classically portrayed this situation. An exploratory Earth vessel meets a similar alien ship by the Crab Nebula. Terrified of being followed and having their home world destroyed as a precautionary act, neither dare leave, yet neither wishes to fight. In the end, spurred on by a discovery of a fundamental kinship shown rather bathetically by the sharing of 'dirty stories', they devise the method of exchanging ships, taking care to destroy all detection devices and clues to the location of their home worlds and arranging to meet in a year's time in the same place for trade.[34]

Wells' Martians of *The War of the Worlds* are in the category of aliens who are hostile and yet genuinely different, as are those of Van Vogt's *The War against the Rull* (1959). Mostly, however, they are very akin to humanity – even the exquisite hostile butterflies of Vernor Vinge's *A Fire upon the Deep* (1992) – if only in the way they think. The unquestioned assumption is that sentience is universal and thus identical, even if bodily forms are not.

There are exceptions to this. The New Zealander Philip Mann has been commended for the 'alienness' of his aliens, notably the 'enigmatic' Pe-Ellians of *The Eye of the Queen* (1982).[35] Such aliens may not only be incomprehensible to us (ineffable) but also indifferent. Those in Clarke's early *Rama* books show a sublime disinterest in the concerns of humanity. This may be – as there – as great a blow to our self-esteem as to find neighbours utterly beyond us in technological sophistication or 'spiritual' development, let alone ones worried enough about us to want to blot us out. The Kybers of Ian Watson and Michael Bishop's *Under Heaven's Bridge* (1981) are representatives of a whole school of sf aliens who remain insolubly enigmatic. Not only looking different but thinking differently too, their behaviour reaches beyond human rational grasp.

The apparently sentient vegetations of Ursula Le Guin's 'Vaster than Empires and More Slow' (1971), the ocean in Stanislaw Lem's *Solaris* (1961), the self-organizing, inorganic, metallic swarming crystals of the same author's *The Invincible* (1964) all represent imaginative cravings for the 'unknown, perhaps the unknowable'. Here are combined the desire for contact and a 'haunting sense of confrontation with it'.[36]

Alien redeemers

As we have already identified, the dominant modern model is that of aliens as saviours. Whilst aliens can be shown as masters, cosmic stooges, indifferent sharers of the same stage, in general treatment of them tends to polarize to opposite extremes – the monstrous efficient killing machines of *Alien* (1979, and successors) and *Predator* (1987), versus the delightfully vulnerable grotesques of *Close Encounters* and *E. T.* Either way, nausea results: the consequence of mayhem on the one hand, mawkishness on the other. Most modern aliens (with the exception of the delightfully witty *Mars Attacks*, 1996) are not merely nice; they come to redeem, to lead humanity to the stars. Space is still the goal, escape from the prison of Earth the aim. The aliens are Gnostic deliverers, bringers of hope and the saving knowledge. They are not just technologically more sophisticated than us; they are morally better.

This is an old theme in science fiction, going back to Clifford Simak's soft-edged mid-Western lyricism. In 'Kindergarten' (1953) benevolent aliens 'demonstrate a technique for reducing all military weapons to impotence and incidentally, but quite predictably, heal the hero's cancer'.[37] The story ends with the main character and his girlfriend in a classroom: 'Side by side, they sat down, waiting for the Teacher'. In the award-winning *Way Station* (1963), a lonely farmer is made immortal by extraterrestrials as payment for his willingness to act as 'station-master' for a galactic teleportation system. In the climax to the story, a mysterious stolen alien artefact is discovered at his 'way station', bringing mystical awe, love and redemption to the whole galaxy as well as to Earth.

Amis comments on such aliens that through beings of this 'unconscionable niceness', 'emotions of humility and reverence most commonly make their appearance in science fiction and I should not fight hard against a diagnosis of these as religious or at least religiose'.[38] John Griffiths similarly writes:

'Stories about [aliens] by Western SF writers reveal three things: an ineradicable instinct for colonisation, an insatiable curiosity about the nature of man himself, and a great sense of loneliness . . . above all, I believe, [sf about aliens] reveals a sense of loneliness, however dignified, which is bound to descend on man without religion'.[39]

Simak's romanticism is typical of that longing,[40] as is his linking of it with our own sense of inadequacy. Aliens (if there be such!) thus are seen as redeemers. Others may eschew this as feebly weak-minded, a demonstration of despair and lack of faith in humanity's own ability to redeem itself. Yet these views (of human self-dependence and of alien saviours) exist side by side in writers such as Arthur C. Clarke. *2001*, for all its loving evocation of human technological achievement is fundamentally a story of alien supervision a million years old; humanity is led on to become an apprentice godling. As here, so in *Childhood's End* (1954):

> The man who in sf is often seen as standing for the boundless optimism of the soaring human spirit, and for the idea that there is nothing Man cannot accomplish, is best remembered for the image of mankind being as children next to the ancient, inscrutable wisdom of ancient races . . . . There is something attractive, even moving, in what can be seen in Freudian terms as an unhappy mankind crying out for a lost father; certainly it is the closest thing sf has yet produced to an analogy for religion, and the longing for God.[41]

Conclusion: fellow-creatures

An alternative model again would see aliens as fellow-creatures in a universe greater than both of us. Early examples are the Martian Tweel of Stanley Weinbaum ('A Martian Odyssey', 1934) and Raymond Z. Gallun's 'Old Faithful' (also 1934) who resembles a starfish and is unimaginatively entitled Number 774, but nevertheless is loved by the scientist hero and his fiancée who declare him human – 'human in everything but form'. Similarly, Kirk says of Spock that: 'of all the souls I have known his was the most . . . human'.[42] Is this human imperialism? Is the assumption that aliens are only valuable if they are like us? Or is it that they too are recognized, to use C. S. Lewis' phrase from his 'outer space' trilogy, as 'hnau', rational beings (and thus, in Lewis' thinking, made in God's image)? Such are the hrossa, seroni and pfifltriggi of his *Out of the Silent Planet*. In Lewis' version of events, as we have seen, aliens are more likely to be our victims than either our saviours or our destroyers.

Are aliens then master, saviour or fellow-creature? Indeed is it really possible to understand what it means to be a creature without acknowledging belief in a Creator? A belief in someone above us all relativizes our perception of our own and other species. The shift to either extreme, monster or hero, tends to occur otherwise – either that or the whole of life itself is divinized, and thus all expressions of it (also a popular move). This tends to lose critical focus since culture becomes beyond rebuke – hence the increasing romanticization of the violent Klingons in *Star Trek*, and the ludicrous situations created by the 'Prime Directive'.

In any case, sf provides its own witness of eternity in the stars themselves. Their beauty has come to stand for the 'otherness' of transcendence – what Olaf Stapledon in *Star Maker* calls 'the cold light of the stars, symbol of the hypercosmical reality'.[43] It is difficult for anyone with sensitivity to look through a telescope and not be moved by its beauty. Yet, at the same time, it is still part of creation – like us.

The Christian viewpoint is here at odds with that of science fiction. Neither humanity, nor aliens, nor the universe need to be divinized for there is already a God. All three are alike creatures. The dividing line is not between us and aliens, or us and the universe (with infinity, immortality ascribed to one or the other), but rather between God and all that is not God – that is, the traditional distinction between Creator and creature. It is entirely understandable and natural that, in a genre which methodologically rejects the existence of God, one part of creation is given his role. But it is wrong.

Chapter 9

A lonely universe

She didn't know she had died.

She had, in fact, died twice – by accident the first time, but suicide later.... A line of nuns floated by overhead.... They were riding the magnetic line at the axis of the city cannister, as graceful as small ships. It was a common enough sight, even a homey one.

But then Rebel's perception did a flipflop and the nuns were unspeakably alien, floating upside-down against the vast window walls that were cold with endless stretches of bright glittery stars embedded in night.

(Michael Swanwick)[1]

Alternatives in identity

Few books in science fiction start in so confusing a way as Michael Swanwick's *Vacuum Flowers* (1987). To start with there is death – a difficult enough topic for us normally. We are told in an offhand manner that the protagonist has somehow survived it – not once but twice. Then we have a supposedly familiar scene ('nuns'), expressed in such a way as to make it seem extremely odd ('floating'). But we are told this sight is familiar, 'homey' to the protagonist ('Rebel'), till her perception (not ours!) does a 'flipflop' and it seems alien. At this point, we begin to locate ourselves. We are in space, the nuns are floating ('upside-down') because there is no gravity, and we are probably in a specially designed space habitat; this means we are in the future, probably the relatively distant future. The survival of death is probably something technological. Correct on all points. Things have changed, but there are still points of reference.

96

Some sf or fantasy books start with the familiar and lead on to the increasingly strange (thus Wells and C. S. Lewis). *Vacuum Flowers*, like Stanislaw Lem's *Return from the Stars* (1961) goes the other way. It wants to make us feel lost. It succeeds. The story of Rebel Elizabeth Mudlark (her improbable full name) is set in a future time of orbiting city cannisters and hollowed out asteroids, small specialized cybernetic and bioengineered colonies floating between the planets. In this world everything is available for a price. Violence and crime are rife. Society oscillates between anarchic individualism and ruthless corporate manipulation: only the fittest survive.

In this complex world, identities can be shared by 'wetware', specialized software indicated by facepaint. The original Rebel Mudlark died in space but her identity was salvaged from her body by a wetware corporation and tried out on Eucrasia Walsh, one of a growing number of 'persona bums' used for field-testing new programming. Preferring Rebel's identity to her own, Walsh attempted to destroy both her own mind and the master copy of Rebel's persona – keeping the only copy for herself. Now the company is after her, either to recover its sullied merchandise or destroy it in order to maintain its reputation. Eucrasia Walsh with Rebel Elizabeth Mudlark's mind is now on the run. (Dualism, again, please note.) Will Rebel's personality 'take' in Walsh's body, or will the latter's memories begin to recover and take her over? The issue is identity.

Rebel is aided by Wyeth, a character with four distinct personalities – which he switches between. They flee to Mars, then Earth. In contrast to Rebel's resilient identity are 'Shadow' and 'Snow', artificial limited intelligences (ALIs), created computer characters with full self-consciousness but lifespans only a tragic few minutes long. As Rebel travels she finds other groups, seeking identity in ways ranging from religious self-abandonment to romantic love.

In addition, two alternative societies are described, both very different to the atomistic vision of the space colonies. One is 'People's Mars' – a collectivist world run by a military dictatorship (the Stalinist-style Stavka), for whom all work on the unified goal of a terraformed Mars. The other is the

Comprise, a vast hivemind, generated through the development of artificial intelligence which has now taken over the Earth. It seeks to expand and absorb all others into itself but its problem is maintaining its unity beyond the Earth's atmosphere. Rebel has the integrity it lacks. Political and individual identity coincide here.

The story follows Rebel's adventures in all these places. Naturally, evil is defeated (mostly) and good conquers. The conclusion produces a dilemma, however. Rebel has the quality of the *Vacuum Flowers* of the book's title, bioengineered weeds that exist in vacuum, feeding off metal. She, like them, is never wholly destroyed. What makes her tick? 'That's just the way I am, I guess', she says.[2] This seems to affirm a given identity we just have to hang on to. The Comprise gives the option of joining a telepathic, vastly intelligent, internally tranquil entity; Mars, that of sacrificing oneself for a utopian project and the general good. Science fiction is unwilling to abandon individuality, whatever the attraction of barrier-destroying relationships. Rebel individualistically asserts her will over Wyeth to get him to do what she wants when their love and perceived duties conflict. Are we not back to the anarchic, corporate society (and the exercise of raw power) with which we began? Is this 'solution' really a solution at all?

Capitalism in space

In many ways, the atomistic individualism of Swanwick's orbiting cities could simply be seen as an extension of Western capitalism into space. This is common, particularly in Western sf. We see this naively in Simak's charming *Off-Planet* (collected, 1988), and more hardheadedly in Frederick Pohl's recent work (*Narabedla Inc.*, 1987, and the *Heechee* series, 1977–), in Larry Niven (the Pierson's Puppeteers of his *Tales of Known Space*) and – as practised by aliens – in Vernor Vinge's *Fire upon the Deep* and Zahn's *Spinneret* (1985). Such commerce is usually conducted with extraordinary objectivity and ruthless self interest. Only Russian sf (e.g., the Strugatsky Brothers) has set out to intentionally offer an alternative. Even where it does appear in Western sf (e.g., the corporatist U.S.C. in Greg Bear's *Beyond Heaven's River*, 1980) it acts merely as a foil to the capitalistic winners.[3]

To a large extent this is mainly because sf is a Western and American phenomenon. For Marxist critic H. Bruce Franklin, Robert A. Heinlein above all represents *America as Science Fiction*. When his critical study with this title (1980) was awarded a Science Fiction Research Association (SFRA) Pilgrim award in 1983, there were some angry responses. The book is described by Leon Stover as 'of more interest to American-hating Marxists than to students of American science fiction', Heinlein's fault being that he had 'the confidence to assert the fundamental values of American culture, for all its failings; on the unabashed premise of its basic superiority'.[4]

Heinlein is particularly interesting, because of what critics have described as his divided mind. His 'Logic of Empire' (1941), set on Venus, argues depressingly that slavery is sometimes inevitable, given the nature of economics. Two of Heinlein's most attractive works, *Citizen of the Galaxy* (1958) and *Double Star* (1956) also deplore slavery and corruption whilst being simultaneously resigned to them. His best-selling *Stranger in a Strange Land* (1961) has a gospel of free love and anti-establishment rhetoric that won disciples from hippies to Charles Manson; on the other hand, *Starship Troopers* (1959) depicts with enthusiasm a military training that borders on brainwashing. It too generated a response – Harry Harrison's savage satire *Bill, the Galactic Hero* with its unforgettable recruiting sergeant Deathwish Drang (1965). There is a strange paradox at the heart of Heinlein's thinking for all his 'wolfish and thoroughgoing' view of liberty ('it boils down to what a man can grab for himself')[5]: 'Man is an animal, in his view, and a dangerous one, who must fight. He can unite and cooperate only when he has a common enemy. Thus military organizations are ideal models for human societies.'

On the other hand, however: 'Heinlein loves a story of individuals triumphing over a system .... His social ideal is a tightly organized hierarchy .... But his ideal individual is a totally free man, which means that his heroes fit awkwardly into his ideal societies.'[6]

By turns Heinlein can expound in all seriousness ruthless Social Darwinism (*Beyond This Horizon*, 1942), racism (*Farnham's Freehold*, 1964) and sexual self-indulgence (all his later work). The Martian Messiah of *Stranger in a Strange Land* (1961) taught on the one hand a gospel of free love and 'grokking', but was also inclined to 'discorporate' people who irritated him.[7]

The letters of Robert Heinlein's name were rearranged by the mischievous John Sladek as 'Hitler I. E. Bonner'.[8] His 'rugged social philosophy' of 'TANSTAAFL' ('There Ain't No Such Thing as a Free Lunch') provoked Harlan Ellison to physically attack a fan wearing a TANSTAAFL badge at a convention.[9]

Yet, for all this, Heinlein is inconsistent. If individualism is so satisfying, why does he so often search for transcendence, for group loyalty or merging that go beyond the atomistic self? If he holds an inherent tension in his thought, maybe he represents not just American but much modern political thought as well. It is clearly one that has strong affinities with Swanwick's vision too.

Loneliness

Sf's stories on telepathy reveal not just the search for enduring identity but also its longing to transcend loneliness. Swanwick's three alternatives in *Vacuum Flowers* speaks for many. Sf author Jack Williamson writes: 'we are all born screaming egomaniacs. Yet, never born alone, we can't exist alone . . . life is an endless series of uncertain compromises between the drives of the self and those unending social demands'. For Williamson, H. G. Wells' life exemplified 'the universal conflict between individual and society'.[10]

On a collective scale, the same thing applies to the human race. Are we alone? Are there any others? On the one hand, humanity in heroic solitude bestrides the stars; on the other hand, we want someone else to talk to!

This individualism is particularly evident in disaster stories, like the post-holocaust scenarios of Greg Bear and Joe Haldeman. Already in the latter's *The Forever War* (1975) there is despair both at the nature of humanity and the structures of the universe: it is perhaps not accidental that the earlier notorious 'Puritanism' of science fiction is replaced here by a dehumanizing brutal casualness about sexual matters. Haldeman's other books, such as *Worlds* (1981) and *Worlds Apart* (1983), are similar both in their depiction and acceptance of promiscuous sexual behaviour (both hetero- and homosexual), and in their dismal view of the human future.

So often we see a sexual or romantic liaison which becomes ultimately insignificant in the light of the necessity to preserve the individual amidst the morally annihilating destruction of everything – it is merely a case of *égoisme à deux*, helpful but not constituent of personal being. Ultimately one is alone.

Such catastrophe was quite likely to be depicted in science fiction of the past, but, as Amis put it, did not need to 'be explained as pessimism or fatalism, rather as a plot-manoeuvre for setting up a story about mutation, or tribal society'. Though Frederick Pohl was always a rather depressed spectator of the future, the world of *Gateway* (1976), the first book of the *Heechee* series, is more dismal than most, concentrating on the grim personal consequences of interstellar travel. Rather like Boris Pasternak's *Doctor Zhivago* (1958), we have the depiction of individuals endeavouring to lead human, loving lives in an aggressively hostile environment. As with Haldeman, this is a climate that wars against humanity. Pohl's characters now seem remorselessly, ruthlessly alone, dependent on no one but themselves, on nothing but their own resources; the characters may feel compassion but it comes a poor, if regretted second, to the necessity for individual survival.

In the 1950s, Kingsley Amis wrote of what he called the 'boundless self-confidence' of science fiction, 'a feeling that if humanity to itself do rest but true, no situation will be too tough and no problem too difficult'.[11] In writing these words, we can now see, he was reflecting the pre-Vietnam situation of his times. Often now, however, even in the more traditional science fiction writers, we meet a profound melancholy.

Being persons

What are the conceptual roots of this extreme individualism we have noted which at the same time, aware of its inadequacy, often cries out for redemption? It is typical of its Enlightenment source which elevated the single human subject, asserting the primacy of human reason. In this it was true to the ancient Greek tradition of rationalism in which the discarnate intelligence is thought to be able to comprehend the universe. Within the dualistic tradition, mind or soul is separate from body or corporeality and is superior to them, being eternal. The truth of the universe can be mentally beheld and thus comprehended. All is graspable. Reality is fundamentally mental.

The nineteenth-century idealist philosopher Hegel replied to the all embracing cosmologies of Plato and Plotinus with his own synthesis of reality which claimed to be able to comprehend everything within its boundaries. In vain did its opponents like Søren Kierkegaard complain of being themselves sucked into the system, of being treated as footnotes in it.[12] Such a mental vision of reality, complained Kierkegaard, claimed that reality could be thought; for him, however this was impossible, a colossal piece of human arrogance: it could not be thought, only lived.

Similarly, modern philosophers like John MacMurray[13] have rejected the Cartesian definition of the person as the thinking self. Descartes, with his celebrated maxim, *cogito ergo sum* ('I think, therefore I am') separates the mind – as the true self – from the body, and locates knowledge in the isolated individual. Thus one cannot be sure whether anything material, even one's own body, is real, or whether anyone else has a mind like one's own. It might all be illusion. This is the result of a strict following of methodological doubt. The individual centre of consciousness, is thus *the* subject, *the* individual – a very solipsistic conclusion.

Such an approach makes personal relations dubious at best. The Cartesian model of humanity is a collection of separate distinct individuals like little atoms,[14] wandering around bumping into one another, perhaps, but remaining distinct and separate. As Colin Gunton has pointed out, the

Cartesian scheme annihilates personal relations effectively by holding them to be a second act, successive to a primary state of being.[15]

By contrast with this model, John MacMurray spoke of the human person as an agent, a doer, so that thought does not precede action but accompanies it. Such a being finds his or her identity in personal relationships. This model does not start from doubt (the Cartesian premise) but faith. Cartesianism can neither be proved nor disproved, but niether can this alternative. It is the one we live by in practice. (We do not demand a chair prove its existence before we sit down on it!)

An understanding of personal being as constituted by relationships has been advocated by a growing number of theologians in recent years – not least by Christian theologians who have found in the doctrine of the Trinity not just a model but a basis for such an understanding.[16] In this way of thinking, it is not that first we are individuals and then – as a second act – that we relate with others (the Cartesian model), but that we are persons precisely by being in relationship (rather as God exists as 'three in one' and 'one in three').[17] Theologian John Zizioulas summarizes the idea by saying that we have our being by going beyond our being in 'ecstasy', that is, in being lifted up out of ourselves.[18] It is by forgetting ourselves that we truly become ourselves. The one who seeks to save his or her own life is the one who loses it. In Dietrich Bonhoeffer's famous phrase Jesus is 'the man for others'. Jesus is the only genuine human because, unlike all those in the crowd, he cares only for them. They are all striving to be different and to be themselves, and in this way are all alike – 'the crowd'; Jesus, who renounces all this and lives only for them is the only real one there.[19]

So it is with us: we are who we are as we deny ourselves for others. It is love that makes us human. It is not that we have a choice between individuality on the one hand and acting for others on the other; rather, contrary to both these false alternatives, we are established as true persons only by being related to others in love. I am a husband but only a husband in relationship to my wife; a father but only in relationship to my children. The more I truly am for others, the more I truly am myself. This understanding goes completely against the notion of the world that we have to look after ourselves and only thus do we exist. To 'look out for oneself' is actually a way of committing suicide.

Science fiction writers like Michael Swanwick and Robert Heinlein oscillate hopelessly between the assertion of the individual and the quest to transcend it. The only answer is the genuine love which breaks down the barriers we place around the individual to protect it. This opens the person in vulnerability and allows relationships to make us who we are. But that is the only way. Theology would go further and say that only God can really enable us to open up to one another.

Moreover, relationality operates not just among ourselves as creatures; it is when we are genuinely open to God that we are most human. As Augustine put it in his famous words, 'You have made us for yourself O God, and our hearts are restless until they rest in you'. Humanity does not have existence in itself, but as a creature, directed for and made for God. As humanity realizes and expresses this, it realizes what it is meant to be. To try and be God leads us to suicide. A rebellious humanity raising its hand against God sounds heroic – but it is actually fundamentally stupid. For it is in being *for* God, that we are most for ourselves.

This view is derided by much science fiction as palpably absurd. A humanity relying on its own resources seeks its own being among the stars. Without God, it seeks to be God itself. But such a quest is misplaced, for it ignores the nature of who we are, and what we were meant to be.

Chapter 10

Between two worlds:
Science fiction and postmodernism

> Recipe for Cyberpunk Cake: One cup *film noire*, one cup
> *Bester*, two tablespoons *Blade Runner*..., a dash of
> Delany..., mix thoroughly, cover in a thick layer of
> Reaganesque hype and Ramboesque aggressiveness. Bake at
> full heat for three years, then let simmer. Serves two good
> writers (Gibson and Sterling) and several hangers on.
>
> (Kim Stanley Robinson)[1]

Cyberpunk

In 1984, a new sf author called William Gibson published a
book called *Neuromancer*. In the history of sf, rarely has so
much been written about one book. Gibson was credited
with beginning a new wave in sf, 'cyberpunk' a name which,
thanks to TV and the trendiness of the topic, transcended
the confines of the genre. The word 'cyberspace' which he
coined was bandied around the airwaves as the hottest thing
since sliced bread – along with Apple, CDs, Bill Gates and
'the information superhighway'.

The hero of *Neuromancer* is Case, a 'cyberspace cowboy'.
He plugs his brain into a 'cyberdeck' (a networked computer)
by means of a jack and neurally implanted electrodes. In this
way he gains access to 'cyberspace', 'mankind's unthinkably
complex consensual hallucination'. In this surrealistic 'virtual
landscape', data banks appear like buildings, skyscrapers and
chasms, down which one travels in search of data. Information is everything: cyberpunk is the literature of the age
of information. Case is on the bottom of society, a surfer

105

'who is wise to the movement of the waves, but ignorant about the ocean'.[2] He travels in the urban wildernesses of Ninsei, the underside of Japanese city Chiba, and the Sprawl or BAMA ('the Boston to Atlanta Metropolitan Area'). This is the world of hustlers, crooks and villains.

There are throw-away, background references (usually unexplained) to the detail of a future world dominated by Japanese-style 'zaibatsus' (multinationals), the Yakuza (Japanese Mafia) and powerful manipulative organizations. 'The kaleidoscopic information overload, or "noise" factor, has a surrealistic effect, especially as combined with information gaps and the interweaving of dense plots that a reader can never fully grasp.'[3] References abound to exotica such as neo-Aztec architecture and Kandiniski-look coffee tables. Peculiar religions abound: Rastafarianism and the Haitian Voodoo cult. All this diversity is nevertheless part of a pervasive world culture, dominated by Japanese and German goods. Power and government is remote and alien to the street denizens.

Case moves through the urban undergrowth, seeking to use his skills and make money. On the way he picks up Molly, a 'street samurai' with retractable scalpel blades under her nails and surgical eye implants. He comes to work for 'Wintermute', an AI (Artificial Intelligence) which has become self-aware and is ruthlessly using human beings in its search for self-transcendence (the usual story here, but Gibson started it). The climax of the story comes with Case's illegal penetration of an orbiting satellite city database and his perilous cyberspace journey through its lethal ICE (intrusion countermeasure electronics).

Gibson describes his inspiration as 'watching kids in video arcades'. Here we clearly see the fictionalization of virtual reality, the internet, visual icons. 'Cyberpunk' in some ways represents a belated gesture in the direction of computers on the part of science fiction. Yet *Neuromancer* is traditional enough to have its computers attain artificial intelligence. The computer emphasis mixes with the urban nightmare, leading to another name for the subgenre, 'technosleaze', 'tales of mean streets and microchips'.[4]

Cyberpunk is described as having 'created a "postmodern"

form that epitomized for the first time the human, or post-human, impact of computer technology and its ability to create virtual realities'.[5] If, in the 1970s the sf text *par excellence* was Ursula Le Guin's *The Dispossessed* (with attention paid to Philip K. Dick) then Gibson's *Neuromancer* became the text of the 1980s. In this light it is entertaining to read that when Gibson wrote *Neuromancer*, he knew almost nothing about actual computers. It has been suggested that 'its computer-conscious author has been exposed as a man who never progressed beyond the type-writer and returned his first word-processor on the grounds that, when he switched it on, "it just buzzed and flashed lights at him"'.[6]

So, is *Neuromancer* postmodern? It is certainly depressing. As John Clute points out, Gibson refuses 'to countenance any normal science fiction sorting-out of the world'. Rather than being about world-changing 'conceptual breakthrough', Gibson is more about 'surviving in style'.[7] Cyberpunk breathes an air of surprise: its writers 'did not expect the world to turn out like that . . . they remain shocked that individuals can be so powerless'.[8] Clute writes that it is not so much original as having its finger on the pulse of change with 'the underlying grim sense that surfing the surface is not the same as owning the ocean'.[9]

In the new science fiction, heroes and heroines have given up trying to save the world; the best they can do is to try and save themselves. Lives are carelessly wasted as if we were operating in some kind of Rambo-like wasteland. Getting ahead in one's chosen profession – whether it be as super computer hacker or hitman (there is an extraordinarily contemporary respect for the expertise of assassins) – is all that counts. Relationships are merely incidental, oases, punctuating with some kind of brief nourishment the emptiness of the surrounding desert. There is a craving for love, and a sense of yearning and loss, but no fulfilment.

The one thing that drives the hero to rage in *Neuromancer* is love. It is his girlfriend Linda Lee's feeling that he has failed to love her that leads her to betray him. Yet when she is killed she is just 'cooked meat'.[10] The expression 'meat' is repeated time and again through this novel referring not just to dead bodies but to the flesh which may distract the cowboy. It points to the new dualism enabled by cybernetics – the escape of the mind from the body to a world without limit. Case's journeys into 'the Matrix' are described as a disconnection of his disembodied consciousness from the body, the return into 'the prison of the flesh' as a 'Fall'.[11] In cyberspace he meets Artificial Intelligences, the new gods. Information has become divine.

Neuromancer is not unusual in presenting a world in which characters relate to one another simply through particular momentary needs. In many thrillers the main problem is of finding someone to trust. Motives there too are sordid and unclear, identity fragmented and confused, roots thin, figures whirled endlessly from one location to another. Sf here could be argued to be simply catching up with general culture. And if this is so, *Neuromancer's* divergence from previous sf is no more nor less than postmodernism's from modernism as a whole. It has been argued that postmodernism is not so much post-modern as ultra-modern; rather than being innovative, it merely highlights sceptical tendencies that have always been fundamental to the modernist movement. However, the argument goes, the inherent subversion within modernism has hitherto been insufficiently pursued, and when it comes out (rather like the extremes of romantic dissonance in Wagner or Schoenberg's music) it is frequently greeted with horror by more conservative members of the same approach. In science fiction, 'cyberpunk' could plausibly be argued to represent merely a development in the genre, rather than a radical new departure.

Indeed, we have already indicated the extent to which sf from the beginning has been sceptical, even of itself. For every triumph, there has been a disaster; for every achievement, a failure. Could cyberpunk not merely be another expression of that scepticism?

As for the moral nihilism of cyberpunk, its 'sense of moral vacuum',[12] this is hardly unique. If the colour grey dominates Gibson's works, 'suggesting both a moral indeterminacy and a blurring of all realities', then he is not alone.[13] We have already observed the children's comic *2000 AD* with its figures of 'Judge Dredd' and 'Rogue Trooper'. Harlan Ellison's story, *A Boy and His Dog* (filmed in 1975 in mean and depressing mood) is in the same vein: in a world suffering the aftermath of holocaust the hero kills his girlfriend and feeds her carcass to his ailing telepathic dog. John Brosnan and Peter Nicholls describe the story as 'brutally pragmatic'.[14]

Postmodernity and postmodernism

According to postmodernism, there is no good overarching narrative, no universal language. We are condemned to pluralism, or at least to plurality. Truth cannot be known; meaning is not objectively present, but is individually sought and made. We make our own reality.

Most sf is modernistic, in the manner of *Things to Come*. In the words of David Attenborough:

> Science . . . tries to exclude the subjective and, as far as possible concentrate on the objective. The evidence that it seeks must be solid, verifiable and as true in central Siberia as it is in Southampton. Science, simply, is the one element of the human culture that is independent of individual societies and is truly international . . . . In a shrinking world, where, increasingly, all humanity must speak and debate together, science is providing the first truly universal account of humanity's origins.[15]

All this postmodernism denies utterly. Rather it sees science as only one model of reality, as valid as (but no more than) other ways of looking at the universe. Nothing is neutral, not even reason, for it too is a notion of humanity and varies from culture to culture. Thus a universal scientific culture is by definition impossible. The scientific model is based on a typically male equivalence of knowledge with power, leading to an instrumental, anti-ecological view of the universe as lying at our disposal, together with a systematic reduction of the complexity of life to basic particles and fields.[16] It is characterized by a (male) Cartesian concept of disembodied reason, leaving the body behind and getting to know the universe in itself. Science is the only true way of knowing and, if there is any value in anything else, it must subordinate itself to science.

By contrast, much modern science fiction shows an

extended failure of nerve, reflecting the changed position of science in modern society and indeed a subjectivist interpretation of science itself. Rather than assuming in a missionary way that all scientific and technological change is for the better, it attempts to discuss what it would be like to live in such a world, and reflects the fragmentation and complexity of our own society and our apparent powerlessness in it.

Humanity and nature

Part of the modernist dream is the hope of control, of freeing humanity from dependence on nature to have power over it and our own destiny. Ultimately, the desire is to free ourselves totally from the limitations of the flesh, from death, from contingence, from our existence as creatures. Gibson's 'cyberspace cowboys' continue that dream, leaving the 'meat' behind, attaining a pure realm of thought.

Earlier, the thought of control was thought of in more materialistic ways. Eighteenth-century mathematician and astronomer Pierre Simon Laplace represented this view (an extension of Newtonian classical physics) with his claim that if you could exactly measure the position of everything in the universe, working its further movements out to eternity would only be a matter of doing the sums. Knowledge led to control. The vision of a humanity controlling the universe, exercising its mind over the universe's matter, beckoned.

Michael Crichton's book *Jurassic Park* (1990), and Steven Spielberg's 1993 film of it, are an attempted refutation of this viewpoint. Humanity knows so much about DNA that it can bring back from extinction dinosaurs and put them in a theme park, 'controlling' them. Crichton spends a lot of time detailing these controls and refers repeatedly to the 'Control Room'. But they do not work. The dinosaurs get loose; control fails. The story oscillates between the rapidly disintegrating illusions of the 'Control Room' and the awesome, irresistable nature rampaging outside.

Actually the knowledge has been 'fiddled'. The wrong plants are being used. Gaps in the DNA chain have been imaginatively filled in, with catastrophic results. 'How can we have the slightest idea what to expect?' asks a doubter to the dismay of the project organizer. The constructors of this grandiose project simply don't know enough and, so the logic goes, they never could know enough.Crichton uses chaotic mathematics (in the shape of the black-clad Malcolm) as a postmodernist wedge to bring crashing to the ground the delusions of modernism.[17] Not only, he prophesies, will the attempt to control the dinosaurs not work, but it cannot work in principle. 'What you're attempting here is not possible . . . life will not be contained'. The attempt shows a 'staggering lack of humility before nature'. Knowledge and control both fail: 'You *never* have control. *That's* the illusion', says one of the critics.

Meanwhile dinosaurs run rampant. Humanity is knocked off its godlike perch and 'Life' replaces it. Humanity's attempt is arrogant for, so it is said, it attempts to defy evolution. If evolution has 'selected' dinosaurs for extinction it is profoundly dangerous for humanity to attempt to reverse the decision. The book suggests that humanity has written its own epitaph: dinosaurs spread to the mainland; humanity's doom is now just a matter of time.[18]

Yet this is all very traditional. The question: 'What have we done?' is the same one raised by Dr Frankenstein, by the maker of Capek's robots, by Oppenheimer at Los Alamos on the morning of 16 June 1945. What have we done? And can we survive it? God is absent, we are on our own.

Absurdism

In this century general Western culture, and sf with it, has seen growing uncertainty about the possibility of knowing and the nature of being: the two major philosophical categories. They are the two major concerns of Philip K. Dick who is thus also exposed as a 'postmodernist' writer. Yet that element has always been part of sf – the ambiguity of a world without God: pride or despair. In a way, modernism represents pride, postmodernism despair.

This is partly evidenced in sf by the prevalence in it of absurdism, an attitude which seems to rejoice (from Robert Sheckley to Douglas Adams) in the sheer impossibility of actually knowing or doing anything. It is thus not primarily

humorous, but rather sad; ultimately there is no order nor
any absolute guidelines as to how things are, how they may
be known, nor how we should behave. This outlook asks
whether science's view of the world is any more right than
that of Pratchett's 'Discworld' – which rides through space
supported by four elephants standing on the back of a giant
turtle. Kurt Vonnegut's *Cat's Cradle* (1963) was just one of
the works that threw dust in the face of 'reality'. Nicholls
writes, 'insofar as [changes in modern physics] have been
grasped at all, it is to cause a retreat into subjectivism and
absurdism'.[19] It is in this way, for example, that Patricia
Warrick defends Dick's wilder speculations.[20]

Douglas Adams' *Hitch-hiker's Guide to the Galaxy* became
a cult in the 1980s. His approach is energetic and witty, with
lots of sf 'in jokes'. The original concept – the Earth demolished to make way for an interstellar bypass – is a gigantic
conceit, but it merely starts a series that makes its way across
the universe and backwards and forwards in time. In the
process, the travellers (Arthur Dent wearing a bathrobe, the
paranoid android Marvin, the two-headed President of
the Galaxy, Zaphod Beeblebrox, Arthur's alien friend 'Ford
Prefect') experience the Restaurant at the End of the
Universe, as well as the accidental beginnings of human life
on Earth (the product of a crashed spaceship full of interstellar undesirables).

All very entertaining – and hardly surprising then that the
answer to the question of the meaning of 'Life, the Universe
and Everything' is the mind-numbingly banal 'forty-two'. It
is equally ludicrous that when the question is laboriously
located it turns out to be 'What is six multiplied by nine?'[21]
This just proves, what we had always suspected, that the
whole thing was a disaster.

Yet absurdism is also accompanied by rationalism. When
someone is put in the 'Total Perspective Vortex', they go
mad. This is because: 'When you are put into the vortex
you are given just one momentary glimpse of the entire
unimaginable infinity of creation and somewhere in it a tiny
little marker, a microscope dot on a microscope dot, which
says "you are here".'[22]

In other words, the one thing humans cannot afford is a

sense of proportion. This is a big departure from the old model of the universe which saw it as our home.[23] Yet it is the logical outcome of an approach which has systematically doubted all there is to doubt. In his book, *The Saviour of Science*, Stanley Jaki not only argues that science is built on Christianity, but it is lost without it.[24] Is something similar true of sf? What is the exact nature of the relationship between Christianity and science fiction?

Chapter 11

Conclusion:
a new foundation

She, the stranger, the foreigner of alien blood and mind . . . shared nothing at all with him, but had met him and joined with him wholly and immediately across the gulf of their great difference: as if it were that difference, the ali-enness between them, that let them rest, and, in that joining together, freed them.

(Ursula Le Guin)[1]

If we consider our contemporary situation, we find that in all areas of life the unique characteristic of modern times con-sists in fact that we are everywhere asking for something that is 'new'. The modern world is modern precisely because men are fascinated by a future which so far nowhere has taken place and hence will be new. This is everywhere the case – with the exception perhaps of the church. Here hardly any-thing new happens . . .

(Jürgen Moltmann)[2]

Other seas, other shores:
the genuine insights of science fiction

The caricature of 'sf's view of Christianity' is that all reli-gion evidences a psychological immaturity which can be, and fortunately is being, replaced by the rationality of a humani-ty come of age. Similarly, according to 'Christianity's view of sf' the genre evidences the ambiguity inherent in a humanity that no longer believes in God.

Yet, if this is all that is said, it is inadequate. The relation-ship goes deeper: science fiction is not merely to be explained away by Christian theology according to criteria that serve only to dismiss and 'place' that which is threatening and different.

Sf raises our eyes from our own concerns to a wonder at the universe, its vast extent in time and space, its extraordinary variety, its exciting challenge, its adventurous strangeness. As we discover new things about it, we are filled with astonishment. Whether it be the genesis of stars in swirling gas clouds and the origin of primeval life, sf takes this aspect of science and popularizes it. For this, gratitude is the only proper response. We can become too introverted and self-concerned. In Tolkien's *The Lord of the Rings* one of the characters in dire peril is given a momentary lift as he sees the stars and realizes there are things forever beyond the evil Sauron's reach.[3] Similarly sf enables us to widen our vision, if only in seeing there is more to God's creation than we imagined.

The human being is all too often conceived in Christian circles in terms of a narrowly 'spiritual' definition – moral behaviour, inward devotional states, attendance at church on Sunday, the inward life of the soul. We take refuge from all the 'changes and chances of this life', the rush and bustle of living in a city by moving into a quiet church. There is indeed something to commend this! Yet if it is based on an idea that God exists in timeless eternity, the world of time is abandoned to perish by itself. The Church then offers a way out of the real world rather than a way of engaging with it. If sf tends to exalt time, change, the material universe and the future too uncritically, the answer is still not to flee from this world of change and alteration to a timeless static eternity. Here Christians need to think sharply about the real meaning of their own faith with its emphasis on a God who becomes incarnate in time and space. Does this not actually mean that time itself is of value, that it is redeemed?

Sf's emphasis on change and alteration takes seriously the place of humanity in creation. It can be demeaning to the goodness of God's creation and God's purposes for humankind to ignore or merely deplore human activity and ability. The notion found in the contemporary Scottish theologian, Thomas F. Torrance, for example, of humanity as 'the high priest of creation' needs attention. In the book of Genesis humanity is given the role of creation's steward. We serve God in this model by caring for creation, understanding it and bringing it to self-expression. Thus caring for the earth is not merely a matter of prudentially 'keeping our own nest clean', but of having responsibility for species that are not our own and do not exist simply for our own sake (which latter concept is a very anthropocentric and ultimately ego-tistic). Creation belongs to God and it does not simply exist to serve us.[4]

We are not alone!

> The otter sat up on its haunches and looked at him. Its eyes were dark, shot with gold, intelligent, curious, innocent. 'Ammar', Shevek whispered, caught by that gaze across the gulf of being – 'brother'.
>
> (Ursula Le Guin)[5]

Sf shares with Christianity in theory at least a delight in otherness. This can take place at a variety of levels. In Eric Frank Russell's *Men, Martians and Machines* (1955) we meet simple infectious joy. The stories in this collection tell of a mixed crew of interstellar explorers (humans, animals, robots) encountering a bewildering diversity of alien worlds. Invention and play run riot. In Chad Oliver's *The Shores of Another Sea* (1971), by contrast, we investigate the meaning of 'alienness'. In this tale set in Africa, the child of a visiting American anthropologist family is kidnapped by aliens who have 'taken over' the baboons they are studying. The power of this story lies in its complexity of layers: in addition to the obvious alienness of the nonhuman visitors from another star, there are equally powerful undercurrents – the ineffable alienness of Africa itself, the baboons (as other creatures on this Earth) and even the children themselves. Unexplained otherness – as the book's title shows – is central to the story.

Lastly, there is the profound delving of Ursula Le Guin into this theme. One of her main ideas is summed up by words of Julian May: 'it is the way of both our races to need the beloved other. Not to strive alone'.[6] The alien is a major concern in all of Le Guin's works, with the critical point being the possibility of contact, of transcending the self in encountering the other. In *Rocannon's World* (1966), the pattern is set. A human marooned on a primitive planet struggles with his situation but, as he gives himself to it, settles and marries, he becomes its saviour – and it is named after him. In a similar way, *Planet of Exile* (1966) describes the encounter of yet more technically-advanced Terrans, colonists who only survive by merging with the natives they have previously despised. In 'Vaster than Empires and More Slow' (1971) and *The Word for World is Forest* (1972), 'a kind of union is gained through human surrender to otherness, and alienation is imaged as violence, madness and raving egoism'.[7] Alienation is seen by Le Guin as the refusal of the alien and the attempt to live solely in the self. To try to construct a universe totally round one's own being, and in accordance with it, is ultimately self-destructive.

Le Guin, like Chad Oliver, is interested in the places where 'otherness' is met on Earth too. For her the male–female relationship is fundamental. Alienness of species and alienness of gender mix in Le Guin: 'he searched for the alien, the stranger, his wife'.[8] She writes in another story of the heroine meeting her husband after a long gap and, seeing him asleep, reflecting: 'Nothing, no distances, no years, can be greater than the distance that's already between us, the distance of our sex'.[9] That difference is liberating, joining and defining at the same time.

Such a communion represents that fellowship across the borders of being for which sf so often strives, but here it is depicted as under our noses if we have eyes to see.

In 1964 Walter Sullivan published a book about the possibility of extra-terrestrial life called *We Are Not Alone*. This title was duplicated on some of the advertising posters for Spielberg's first sf movie, *Close Encounters of the Third Kind*. The same message was given in a poster for *E.T.*: an alien's hand stretches out to touch a human hand, an illustration based on Michelangelo's painting of the creation of Adam on the ceiling of the Sistine Chapel.[10] The message is clear: God has been replaced by aliens.

The desire for us 'not to be alone' is, as we have seen, very strong in science fiction. What Christians offer, by contrast, is a further response to the 'problem' of solitude. Rather than thinking of aliens, fellow-creatures with us in the universe, Christianity proclaims a God who has put us in it. Even if there are aliens (which is by no means a certainty: after all, we still haven't seen any!), this is irrelevant to the bigger issue. Is there a Creator who has made everything in the universe, both us and any other race that happens to exist?

From a Christian point of view, the desire to have fellow-creatures in the universe can be seen as an attempt to fill the hole created by the absence of God. This is perhaps particularly why such races have been given characteristics traditionally connected with him, the so-called divine attributes.

The Christian viewpoint is that the True Other is God; the many kinds of otherness in sf which can be properly saluted mirror the diversity that actually exists within the one true God, Three-in-One and One-in-Three as he is classically described. All these different kinds of otherness are reflections of God's Otherness. As we exist as God's creatures we are set in the midst of this variation to enjoy it, but to do so on the horizontal level (of creation) is not incompatible with acknowledging the deeper vertical level (of relation to the Creator) who made all and who underlies all.

In a famous description, twentieth-century theologian Karl Barth called God the 'Wholly Other'. This meant he was unimaginable by us, even negatively! (That is, one could not even think of God in terms of what we are not.) Barth later came to think this view was too abstract.[11] However, its strength is the way in which it talks of the 'Godness of God', to use another phrase descriptive of his theology. God is not reducible to any human characteristic, either good or bad. We cannot work towards what God is on the basis of what we already know (or think we know) about the world.

We have already noted the difficulty in sf of conceiving of a genuine other. Is the 'sense of wonder' an illusion, all talk of the other mere projection, a 'mirror' of ourselves and our concerns? If God really comes to us, by contrast, the knowledge we receive of him is genuine. We encounter a real Other, not invented by us to fill a gap in our knowledge, but really new, coming to us from beyond our previous experience, who gives that knowledge to us. What this means, therefore, is that what sf seeks, Christianity actually provides. In the words of St Paul at Athens: 'what you worship as unknown, this I proclaim to you' (Acts 17.23).

Again, the problem with the 'mirror' school of thinking is that we do not receive from sf the kind of knowledge of ourselves that a genuine outside perspective would bring. We are like a cat chasing its own tail. Self-reflection only enables us to see what we already know. Our flaws prevent us from seeing deeply in any case. We all know people who cannot see things about themselves that all their acquaintances instantly recognize. The genuine view 'from outside' is needed. Sf's view from outside is bogus, as our examination of Stapledon indicated. A genuine view is what Christianity claims to provide in the person of Jesus Christ. He is the genuine Other who comes into our world, into our space and time to reveal to us both who God is and who we are too. The aim of sf to know ourselves (mirror) is thus answered simultaneously with the aims of encountering the other (wonder) – and indeed by means of the encounter with the genuine Other! It is only because Christ is genuine Other that he can tell us about ourselves. Indeed, we attain that much desired attribute of science fiction, conceptual breakthrough – a new and true way of looking at the universe and at ourselves. Sf invents – in fiction; this is real – in fact.

Sf shares the religious quest. It strives for the transcendent to give us perspective. Christianity, however, is not the way of religion but its contradiction. It is about revelation, not about projection. The way in which God gives us perspective is by coming to us. The fourth-century theologian Athanasius made a vital distinction between 'theology' and 'mythology'.[12] According to this, theology is language 'about' God based on the language 'of' God – that is, given to us by God so that we may speak about him accurately. Mythology, by contrast, consists of stories we invent off the top of our own heads to try and make sense of a puzzling universe. Sf is the mythology of our 'scientific' age: like mythology in all times and places, it has sought to interpret humanity's relationship to itself, the universe, the 'gods', life 'after death'. Such stories, such ideas are basically wild guesses, leaps into the void which hope (with ill-based confidence) to make some contact with reality. This is true of the great Greek myths but no less of any kind of thinking which speculates about the unknown, whether described as 'myths' or not.

In Plato's *Phaedo* the Greek thinker Socrates says there is no certain knowledge of what lies (if anything) on the other side of death; no divine word comes from there. The best one can do, suggests his disciple Simmias, is to make a frail barque out of human notions with which to sail through life. However, according to the Christian gospel, a divine Word has indeed come from there: Jesus Christ has been raised from the dead, and speaks to us with confidence of what lies beyond.[13] Moreover, as God, he declares it to us in person.

If sf strives for heaven, Christianity speaks of a heaven who has come among us – but maybe not quite the heaven we had in mind. According to orthodox doctrine, Christ is both fully human and fully divine, not partly one and wholly the other, but both simultaneously and completely. He is truly human; that is, he is good. In him, we see who we are meant to be; in his light, we see we are not like that and are ashamed (or ought to be!). We know ourselves 'by reflection'. In a moment of blinding realization, Jesus' disciple Peter exclaimed, 'Depart from me, for I am a sinful man, O Lord' (Luke 5.8). Yet, though Jesus was the Light of the world, people 'loved darkness rather than light, because their deeds were evil' (John 3.19). Therefore they killed him. They could not bear the truth. But he rose from death; his truth cannot be defeated; he continues to tell us who we are. As John Calvin said, knowledge of God and knowledge of ourselves are intricately bound up together.[14]

This Other comes from the future. Here we are not dealing with extrapolation of the new, but with the genuinely new. There is a vital difference between the predictions of extrapolation and the authentic *novum*. Extrapolation seeks to imagine the future on the basis of the present. It takes tendencies which are now apparent, even if to a small degree, and tries to imagine how they might develop in the future. Yet, as has been suggested already, many of the vital changes happening now are not visible to us. The genuinely new scientific discovery with drastic technological and social economic and political consequences often comes completely unheralded.

This is the distinction made by the theologian Jürgen Moltmann between what he calls *futurum* and *Zukunft*.[15] *Futurum* is the continuation of the present, imaginable from within it; *Zukunft* is that which comes to us from the future as genuinely new – the *novum*. As Moltmann indicates, much Christian thought has emphasized the past; however, it has never ceased either to speak of the last days, the hope of the future activity of God, of what is called in Christian theology 'eschatology'. As Israel looked to the coming of the Messiah, so we too look for the fulfilment of God's Kingdom.

How does this affect our thinking about science fiction? It does so because *futurum* is essentially extrapolation. It can conceive of the future only in terms of the present, of the other in terms of the self, of the unknown in terms of what is already known. It thus has inherent – and quite natural – limitations. It cannot deal with that which is genuinely new, genuinely other. Futurology is thus of its very nature uncertain. As Moltmann insists, the messianic activity of a God coming to us, as it were, from the future (the meaning of the German word *Zu-kunft*, 'coming-to') is not to be comprehended from within the immanent processes of the present world. Even within the limited capacities of our created existence, we cannot accurately anticipate the future.

In theology, by contrast, we have a *genuine* future that comes to meet us from beyond, declaring itself through the person of Christ. This is not of our making but demands that we should rethink our perceptions of the universe on its own terms. This objectivity which comes to us from the future informs us of itself. This is *Zukunft* rather than mere *futurum*.

The hope for Moltmann is grounded on a God who is objectively Other and who comes to us to give us hope. Hope is not constructed from our own perception of our own possibilities, as wishful thinking. Here there is a clear contrast with the messianic claims of modernist science fiction, which so often wants to make humanity its own hero or saviour, and often – by association – the saviour of the universe as well. By contrast, for Christian theology it is Christ who is the Messiah, the one who inaugurates the true Millennium. He is the one who is genuinely Other and who saves us (rather than us saving ourselves).

Stranger in a strange land: a gift to earth

Whilst Christianity is centred around the idea of God giving himself, it is not only in order to be known, but to give us life. We are dealing not only about knowing but about being: God seeks to change us, who we are, not simply what we know. In the crucifixion, Christians believe, Christ's blood was poured out for our sake: he gives his own life for our sake. This is witnessed to the Church in the sacraments of baptism and the Eucharist. In the 'wonderful exchange', so the Fathers taught, 'God became what we are that we might become what he is'; 'he took what is ours and gave us what is his'. God, who is higher than all things, became one of his own creatures to win them back for himself.

This is at odds with the general line of science fiction, in which humanity tries to become God and to cease being a creature. Sf depicts as desirable the renunciation of creature-hood and its many aspects: finitude, mortality, physicality. It yields to the temptation of the Serpent: 'You will not die . . . you will be like God, knowing good and evil' (Genesis 3.4–5). By contrast, the Christian story tells us that God did not think it above him to become human and a creature, and to die. The story of the tower of Babel (Genesis 11.1–9) tells of humanity, swollen with pride, stretching forth its hand to the heavens; Christianity speaks of God becoming one of us.

Sf is fictitious; Christianity is true. Sf invents a 'fabulous' future that dwarfs particularity in cosmos-spanning tales; Christianity is rooted in a real history, in genuine flesh and blood, located at a particular place and time, but still of eternal significance.

In sf, we see humanity's pride and desire for self-realization at all costs; in the incarnation, we see God's humble conde-scension to us and love of us. In sf, creatures ascend to 'pure energy'; in the incarnation, the Word of God (through whom everything was made) becomes flesh. In sf, humanity tries to avoid mortality; in the incarnation, the Son of God comes to die. In sf, humanity seeks for omnipotent power; in the incarnation, the one through whom everything was made screams in agony on the cross. In sf, humans evolve or change into a 'higher form'; in the incarnation, he who is spirit shares in our life and has nowhere to lay his head. In sf, humanity grows to know everything; in the incarnation, the Wisdom of God takes on the measure of a first-century Jewish male. In sf, the enlightened few attain control over the human race; in the incarnation, the Son of God lays down his life for the many so they might be free.

Contrary to Gnosticism, creaturehood is affirmed by Christianity. Eberhard Jüngel once remarked that the reason God became human in Christ was so that humanity and divinity might be definitively differentiated from one another![16] In becoming human God affirms himself as God. In raising us to union with him, he affirms us as creatures and undermines our attempt to be gods. Sf wants to abolish the distinction between Creator and creature, and does so by aspiring to the throne of the Creator. Christianity affirms that creation is good; we are not meant to become something other than what we are, to become non-creaturely or more intellectual, a disembodied spirit, or an android, cyborg or machine. Humans are creatures – and that is good.

In sf the central concern is the death of the universe ('sun-death'); in Christianty it is the death of the Son of God. That does not merely bring to the universe 'survival', an extension of the time of existence (as a reversal of sundeath would) but, rather, transformation to a new mode of existence. We might call this not an addition of time, but a change of it to eternity. Time itself is redeemed. Space does not merely go on for ever, but it too is altered to Heaven.

We are not dealing merely with knowledge, but with something larger than that – with truth that incorporates moral action. As we have seen, there is a strong tendency in sf to exalt intelligence above everything. In Arthur C. Clarke's concluding *Rama* volume (1993), the multivarious universes are seen as a gigantic information-gathering machine. At the very end of the saga the heroine dies, but she is content: she has been given a last-hour tour of the cosmos. 'I will not be afraid because I understand . . . and understanding is happiness', she declares.[17] As with Stapledon, the peace of understanding is God.[18]

A Christian vision is rather different. Information by itself means little. For Christians knowledge and wisdom (deeper concepts) are inseparable from love and moral action. The death of the Son of God comes not merely as a result of the universe's lack of information but from its inhabitants' perversity, their deliberate turning away from the truth. This 'evil' has moral consequences – lying, deceit, jealousy, theft, envy, murder. It leads to the destruction of relationships and of being. It is not merely a matter of ignorance, which can be remedied by 'input'. God's moral 'input' was not heard, but led all the way to the death of a man on a cross at the hands of his fellows. It leads, too, to a salvation undreamed of by those who are its recipients.

The great redistribution

Under God a lot of confused relationships find their place. What is Creator and what is created (and therefore creaturely) are sorted out. God is on the throne of the universe, and humanity and nature (and any hypothetical aliens) are creaturely. Augustine described idolatry as giving worship to that which is made, rather than that which makes. Similarly blasphemy, rather than any discourteous or extreme form of words, is not giving to the Creator the honour due him. Science fiction does both of these.

In the Old Testament idolatry is seen in terms of the worship of natural forces such as wind, earth and sky. Above all, it is observed in the contrast between the worship of Yahweh, the Creator of the universe, the one true God on the one hand, and Baal on the other. Baal is a typical Middle Eastern fertility god, who represents the pattern of nature. The story of the death and rebirth of the seasons follows a cyclical pattern in which Baal heroically fights, is defeated by and finally overcomes the hostile forces of chaos and death.

When the Israelites succumb to Baal-worship, they are giving honour to what is not God, to the created rather than the Creator. What they bow down to is part of the world, of the creation of which they themselves are a part. In giving honour to the imaginary Baal, they also rob God of his due honour as Creator. The biblical account in 1 Kings 17–21 of the conflict between Elijah (as Yahweh's champion) and the priests of Baal portrays Yahweh as the true Lord of the universe, the one who really has control of all the natural elements. He can bring fire from heaven and drench the land in rain, a rain he has previously withheld. He is the God of the earthquake, yet ultimately not identical with it but 'a still, small voice'.

Through the whole of the Old Testament we see this repeated forbidding of the identification of God with anything that is natural. This is so whether that object is an idol created by human hands (the golden calf of Exodus) or something merely to be found in existence – a standing stone, a spreading tree, one of the 'high places' so commonly associated with divinity or, indeed, a star.

Science fiction tends to exalt human fiction and culture and yet it has always had a tendency to worship nature itself as well. Thus, the worship of Gaia and the Sun in David Brin's novel, *Earth* (1990) is entirely logical. At the end of the novel, Gaia awakes to life as a new god (and with its own sign, an encircling motion rather than a cross!) A return to the worship of natural forces goes quite logically with the abandonment of a belief in a transcendent God. We do not worship the maker of all. Instead we worship, in whatever form, ourselves.

We can make the following affirmations. Under God humanity is creaturely – that is, finite and mortal, given an allotted space and time upon this earth. It is physical, material, not a being of 'pure' energy or, indeed, any other kind, versus the pretensions of sf against both of these. Humanity is part of creation and nature, but has a special place in relation to it, contrary to those who would deify either humanity or nature. (This also applies to any hypothetical aliens who might exist.) Humanity's culture is that of creatures – that is, good but limited, and not to be idolized. Its work is not godlike but that of creatures which proceeds within limits. Neither may science be worshipped: it is in the person of Christ that are hidden all the treasures of wisdom and knowledge (Colossians 2.3). Science is 'thinking the thoughts of God after him'; it is not becoming God ourselves. The message of the Psalms and Job still applies: God remains greater than us! The work of humanity, either as technology or as fiction, is only 'sub-creation' (to use

Tolkien's phrase again). It uses the raw material God has created, which should – either in 'fabril' technology or in imaginative fiction - be used within those limits. To a certain extent, as we have seen, it has to be! Neither in knowledge nor in power can humanity create *ex nihilo*, but from the resources of freedom God has given. The Power of God is the Holy Spirit. Humanity may try to usurp 'it', but cannot do so, any more than it can usurp the Wisdom of God in Christ.

St Irenaeus referred to the Word and Spirit as the 'two hands' of God. One might speculate that the knowledge and power claimed for humanity in the modernist paradigm are humanity's ambitious imitation of this, their assault on divinity. Within limits, knowledge and power are analogical to God's being; outside those limits, they threaten to become God himself, displacing him or seizing his throne in his supposed absence.

The desire for freedom

The paradox of 'contingent' human existence is that we are free within certain constraints. Even the play which sf celebrates requires rules. Modern sf oscillates between a desire for absolute freedom on our part and a terror of that absolute freedom in the hands of others where it may be used as power to control us. In Harlan Ellison's, 'I have no mouth and I must scream' (1967), a person, longing to die, is kept alive in torture by an allpowerful entity. There is no escape – the fear of our age.[19] In sf, we so often see the assertion of an abstract Promethean freedom against the odds (and against the contingencies of existence). Always (as in horror) there is the fear that freedom is an illusion, that the human race is irretrievably doomed.

By contrast with all this, Christianity proclaims a freedom in relation for one another under God. It speaks of a paradox of freedom, which depends on God to support it. Our existence as creatures is grounded on the one who made us. God has made us to be free, but it is God who has given us that freedom; consequently, it is when we are most in relation to God that we are most free. We are not free apart from

God; the attempt to be free by ourselves is doomed to failure. Self-dependent freedom is an illusion; the only kind we can have is relational.

The promised land: or 'Beam me up, Scotty'

Mr Spock's motto that 'There are always possibilities' sums up the optimism of most sf. For Ray Bradbury – and despite what he says of humanity destroying itself on earth – space is redemptive. For there humanity will be born again. So too. in Kim Stanley Robinson's *Mars* trilogy. Robinson's pioneers are recreated – 'areoformed' – by Mars (Ares). Like Heinlein (*The Moon is a Harsh Mistress*, 1966) and Ben Bova (*Millennium*, 1976), they will throw off the past and create a brave new world just like the American pioneers. Bradbury too mixes biblical myths of the Garden and the Promised Land with the American myth of the frontier.[20] And, according to Willis McNelly:

> For Bradbury, the final, inexhaustible wilderness is the wilderness of space. In that wilderness, man will find himself, renew himself, and there, as atoms of God, he will live forever. Ultimately, then, the conquest of space becomes a religious quest.... Ultimately the religious theme is the end product of Bradbury's vision of man, implicit in man's nature.[21]

Though Bradbury acknowledges 'the ambiguous promise of the American dream' which in the *Martian Chronicles* ruins two cultures (Earth and the native Martians), nevertheless he declares his belief 'in what we Americans have done to this country, with all the rape that went with it'. In any case, he does not think it will happen again: humanity has grown up.[22]

Thus, as Mogen says, 'the step into space ushers in an awesome new era, not merely from a human perspective but from a cosmic perspective as well, a perspective from which all previous human history appears as merely the final stage of life's bondage to earth ... man enters the space frontier to be reborn, ultimately to be transformed by his new environment'. In Bradbury's story, 'The Rocket Man', light symbolizes the 'overwhelming power of the myth of space, a myth whose origins are ultimately religious but which fuses a religious "sense of wonder" with an evolutionary perspective on man's destiny... the trip is essentially a holy mission'.[23]

Christianity's claim that God has redeemed precisely this world (so we do not need to go anywhere else) seems rather dull by comparison. Yet Christianity's vision is of meeting God, not of becoming God. His presence is Heaven, is Paradise. In God's face we meet eternity, rather than (as in sf) when we ourselves fill space and time. In Christianity, we do not need to do so – the eternal meets us in our world, our home.

Towards a conclusion: stardust and ashes

The service of Ash Wednesday in Lent represents hope – the hope of God acting to redeem us. The old is replaced by the new; both pride and anxiety are burnt away so that self-reliance is replaced by confidence in God. Self-reliance is reduced to ashes – so we can be made clean for God's coming, and trust in him.

In science fiction, by contrast, ashes represent despair, despair at the doom that we may bring upon ourselves through our own stupidity – nuclear ashes. We make, and we break, ourselves.

In science fiction, dust can be seen in two ways – as physical creatureliness, from which condition of weakness we are trying to escape, or (romantically) as our celestial origin or final destiny. 'We are stardust, we are golden, and we've got to get ourselves back into the garden.'

Stardust and ashes in sf thus represents two possible futures awaiting us, one optimistic and glowing (becoming self-transcendent, transforming ourselves and the universe), the other pessimistic and annihilating (destroying the world and ourselves). Here stardust and ashes becomes stardust *or* ashes, a choice of two destinies. As we identified at the beginning of this book, we may get both simultaneously – as in Bradbury. The same science and technology that gives us the stars, can destroy us in nuclear holocaust as well. Stardust and ashes both derive from human technology allied with flawed human nature. Both space travel and atomic energy offer opportunities for triumph and disaster. The problem then is humanity's own being, from which we cannot escape by going into space.[24]

It is a common theme in sf set in the future that we survived to get into space by the skin of our teeth (for example, Brin's *Startide Rising*, 1983). Like various non-human civilizations, we made it through the vitally dangerous period following the discovery of nuclear weapons – just. In one of the *Star Trek* books (*Prime Directive*, 1990), a planet – through being under hostile extraterrestrial influence – annihilates itself, all but wiping out all its inhabitants. This threat – this sword of Damocles – has in reality been hanging over all our heads for fifty years now. The demise of Communism in the form of the Soviet Union has lowered the temperature, setting back the clock hand on the countdown to Doomsday by a few minutes. However, nuclear proliferation continues. Even if there were further massive reductions of nuclear weapons in the former Soviet Union and the USA, an enormous threat would still remain. This is quite apart from the prospect of other countries like North Korea, Iraq or Libya getting the bomb – if they do not have it already. The possibilities for nuclear conflagration in many parts of the world, such as the Middle East, remain strong. Books such as Hal Lindsay's notorious *The Late, Great Planet Earth* (1970), placing Armageddon in the context of international conflict surrounding Israel, remain eerily plausible.

This is only the beginning of a series of possible catastrophes that lie in wait for our planet. The extraordinary growth in knowledge we have seen over the last century or so has enabled us to see back to the first few minutes of creation and detect the microwave background radiation of the Big Bang itself – as well as quasars, pulsars and other distant celestial objects; it has also made possible our self-extinction. Thor Heyerdahl's *Kon-Tiki* expedition of 1948 reports crossing half the Pacific in consistently brilliant clear water; in the *Ra* expedition some ten years later, Heyerdahl comments on rubbish floating even in the middle of the Atlantic. And that was forty years ago! Our planet is threatened by so much now in the way of pollution in air, sea and water, all rendered possible by the incredible advances in science and technology. It is hardly surprising that in many places people are turning against the genie that has brought them electricity, improved health care, better communications, a higher 'standard of living'.

The blunt question is: if humanity is like this, does it deserve to be saved; does it deserve to go on through the galaxy and then the universe, no doubt destroying itself at greater and greater levels of magnitude as it goes (and anybody else unfortunate enough to get in the way as well)? This is C. S. Lewis' crucial and cruel question, to which he gives a resounding 'No' as answer. For him, there is a higher loyalty than our race.

So too in Ursula Le Guin's bitter Vietnam parable, *The Word for World is Forest* (1972) and Lloyd Biggle's ecological 'Monument' (1962, 1974), where the universe has to safeguard itself against a rapacious humanity. In Clarke's 'Before Eden' (1961) the chance of life on Venus is destroyed by garbage micro-organisms left by careless astronauts; in Poul Anderson's 'Sister Planet' (1951) a terraforming plan provokes the hero to slaughter native aquatic Venerians to warn them of humanity's nature. Sf writers too admit: humanity is dangerous.

Is this likely to get better in the future? Scarcely. If we do indeed expand to the stars we will simply be able to destroy more. Peter Nicholls' book, *The Science in Science Fiction* (1982) portrays a number of modestly harrowing proposals for weapons of the future.[25] A gamma ray laser (or 'graser') powerful enough might cause a sun to go nova at many lightyears distance. A 10-tonne spaceship accelerated to 99.99 per cent of light speed hitting a planet would cause a 22 million megaton explosion, smashing continents and stripping away portions of atmosphere.[26] (And should you think there must be some way of stopping such a weapon, please note that a warning message beamed from a watching station on Pluto would take five hours to reach Earth, with the Doomsday machine arriving one fifth of a second later!)

However, this is not the ultimate weapon even within the possibilities we can now envisage: two colliding blackholes, each of 6 kilometres diameter (the same mass as our sun) would cause an explosion of 10 to the 31st megatons of TNT, more energy than our sun will emit over the millions of years of life from its birth to its death. Such an explosion would annihilate solar systems, sterilizing planets of life many light-years distant.

In other words, if we can destroy our own planet within our own technology now, who is to say we will not devise ways of annihilating bigger and bigger ones as we expand into the universe? *Star Wars'* 'death star' may be of quite modest proportions compared to our technological potential.[27]

In Walter M. Miller's superbly ironic *A Canticle for Leibowitz* (1960), humanity recovers slowly from World War III only to destroy itself more thoroughly in another nuclear holocaust. It simply repeats the mistakes of the old humanity. Nothing has changed. It will forever go on the same way, blowing up, destroying, corrupting everything it touches. It shows no sign of being the brave new being that Gene Roddenberry dreams of, one that deserves to travel to the stars. So, what is the answer? Humanity itself must be changed at a fundamental level. In Miller's novel, something new does happen: out of the nuclear holocaust an unfallen creature is born: the innocent Rachel. Here we have an awareness that it is not merely 'what we do' that is the problem, it is 'who we are'. Here we see that 'a new humanity' is required. In Christian terms, this is the humanity we have through Jesus Christ. This is the 'new foundation', the new starting-point that will genuinely lead to a new future.

A human scale

The sf universe leads to pride or despair, through our relationship to it. Are we scared by it or triumphant over it?

Let me end this book which has talked a lot about stories with a story of its own. A *Peanuts* cartoon shows Charlie Brown and Linus under the stars as Linus tells Charlie Brown how big the universe is. Charlie Brown responds: 'I miss my dog.' This gives a human scale to the awesomely huge universe and asks a pointed question (which Carl Sagan would not like) about our values. Is it really true (as *Threads* suggested) that the dilemma of a pregnant girl is insignificant in comparison with nuclear holocaust? Is it really true that human concerns are rendered to a 'pale blue dot' by the vast array of time and space? If God is God, maybe we can regard the universe with awe and be staggered by it, but without feeling reduced to nothing by it either. For those with faith in God, it is neither the field of our triumph or disaster. For the Word of God who – as Graham Kendrick put it – 'threw stars into space', became a human baby.

One of the folders I have been using for this work is entitled 'Fictions of Nuclear Disaster': it contains various apocalyptic, unbelievably depressing enclosures. On its cover one day I discovered some drawings. My daughter had named and drawn pictures of 'Mummy', 'Daddy' and her brother and herself under the bold title: 'God loves us'. God loves us? When we can do such terrible things to ourselves? To some this is illusion, wishful thinking. To others, it is the story of Jesus Christ the crucified and resurrected God. Whatever the disaster, God loves us. What we do is neither the first nor the last word, for we truly rest in the hands of Another.

Notes

Introduction

1. Jeremy Pascal, *The Movies from 1930 to the Present* (London, Hamlyn, 1984), p. 282.
2. Notably *Aniara* (1959) by Karl-Birger Blomdahl, based on Swede Harry Martinson's epic starship poem featuring a computer.
3. John G. Magee Jr, 'High Flight' (Concord, Mass., 1956).
4. Elechi Amadi, *Sunset in Biafra* (London, Heinemann, 1973), pp. 87–8.
5. J. G. Ballard, 'Book Four', Channel Four TV (UK), 24 December 1982.
6. Arthur C. Clarke, quoted by Frederic Pohl at a meeting of the Cambridge University Science Fiction Society, 16 October 1982.
7. Doris Lessing, *Shikasta* (London, Granada, 1981), 'Some Remarks', pp. 10–11.
8. Stephen R. L. Clark, *How to Live Forever: Science Fiction and Philosophy* (London, Routledge, 1995), p. 5.
9. *Church Times*, 10 December 1993, p. 18, quoting the *Sunday Times*.
10. There is a big debate about the nature of story and narrative here. Part of the point is that stories are nonformalizable, and say more than any attempted explanation of them. Accordingly, I have deliberately included quotes, as well as synopses, of sf tales in this book. Janet Martin Soskice (*Metaphor and Religious Language*, Oxford, Clarendon, 1985) argues similarly against Aristotle's notion that metaphors are ornaments which say, in a roundabout way, what could be said better and more clearly if stated directly.
11. Frank Herbert, *The Maker of Dune: Insights of a Master of Science Fiction*, ed. Tim O'Reilly (New York, Berkeley, 1987), p. 61.

133

12. Darko Suvin, *Metamorphoses of Science Fiction: on the Poetics and History of a Literary Genre* (New Haven, Conn., Yale University Press, 1979).

13. Eric Auerbach, *Mimesis*, tr. Willard R. Trask. Princeton, Princeton University Press, 1953.

14. J. T. Como, ed., *C. S. Lewis at the Breakfast Table and Other Reminiscences* (London, Collins, 1980), p. 74.

15. Thus New Zealand sf author Margaret Mahy. As Carl Sagan graphically demonstrates in a chapter grimly entitled: 'The effects of nuclear winter on nations minding their own business', nuclear wars are no respecters of loud proclamations of non-involvement either (Carl Sagan and Richard Turco, *A Path where No Man Thought: Nuclear Winter and the End of the Arms Race*, London, Century, 1990).

Chapter 1 The vast abyss of night

1. *Time*, 20 November 1995, p. 59.

2. Steven Weinberg, *The First Three Minutes* (Glasgow, Collins, Fontana, 1978), p. 61.

3. Nigel Henbest and Heather Couper, *The Guide to the Galaxy* (Cambridge, Cambridge University Press, 1994), p. 131.

4. Peter Nichols, ed., *The Science in Science Fiction* (London, Michael Joseph, 1982), p. 201. 'The most durable of predictions is that of the endless Space Age – the belief that once we have emerged from the cradle of our planet, the future and the universe are ours.' Thus too J. G. Ballard, 'One dull step for man . . .' in *The Observer Review*, 22 December 1996, p. 15.

5. Isaac Asimov, 'Hell-Fire' in *Earth is Room Enough* (1957).

6. John Tusa, 'Killing', episode 8 of *20/20: A View of the Century*, BBC Radio 4, 26 September 1996.

7. Cf. the plan to incarcerate some 30,000 tons of radioactive rail-rods at Yucca Mountain, Nevada, in the biggest hole ever made by humans ('60 Minutes', TVNZ, 1 May 1996). For one sf treatment of nuclear waste, cf. Ben Elton's 1989 novel, *Stark*.

8. E.g. Arthur C. Clarke's 'All the Time in the World' (1952) where a super-bomb test means The End.

9. Such survivalists are depicted as the prime enemies of the rebirth of civilization in David Brin's post-holocaust novel, *The Postman* (1985). This is by contrast to their implicit approval by the right-wing Larry Niven and Jerry Pournelle's *Lucifer's Hammer* (1977) and *Footfall* (1985). The former novel, like Robert Heinlein's *Farnham's Freehold* (1964) also includes black cannibals.

Chapter 2 The sense of wonder

1. Damon Knight, *In Search of Wonder* (1956), (quoted in Peter Nicholls, ed., *The Encyclopedia of Science Fiction: an Illustrated A to Z*, London, Granada, 1979, p. 160).

2. Karl Barth, *Evangelical Theology*, tr. G. Foley (London, Collins, 1963), pp. 61–2.

3. 'Nun rühen alle Wälder', by Paul Gerhardt (*Hymns Ancient and Modern New Standard*, No. 17, words by Robert Bridges).

4. Bob Shaw, 'Light of Other Days' (1966); *Other Days, Other Eyes* (1972).

5. Respectively: James H. Schmitz's 'Grandpa' (1955) and Clifford Simak's 'Ogre' (1943) – vegetable; Ian Watson and Michael Bishop's *Under Heaven's Bridge* (1981) – crystalline; Tweel in Stanley Weinbaum's classic 'A Martian Odyssey' (1934) – silicon; Stanislaw Lem's *The Invincible* (1973) – cybernetic machines; Paul di Filippo's 'Up the Lazy River' (1993) – metallic river.

6. Damon Knight, 'Four in One' (1953); Isaac Asimov, 'Green Patches' (1950); David Masson, 'Mouth of Hell' (1968) and 'Traveler's Rest' (1965).

7. Poul Anderson, 'The Big Rain' (1955); James Blish, 'Bridge' (1952); Clifford Simak, 'Mirage' (1956).

8. Hal Clement, *Mission of Gravity* (1954); Robert F. Young, 'Goddess in Granite' (1957); Isaac Asimov's *Foundation* and Iain M. Banks' *Culture* series.

9. Ward Moore's *Bring the Jubilee* (1953), Keith Roberts' *Pavane* (1968), Philip K. Dick's *The Man in the High Castle* (1962), among many.

10. I. F. Clarke, 'The Future as History' in Rex Malik, ed., *Future Imperfect: Science Fact and Science Fiction* (London, Francis Porter, 1980), pp. 11–25; A. Toffler, 'Science Fiction and Change' in Peter Nicholls, ed., *Science Fiction at Large* (London, Gollancz, 1976), pp. 117–18.

11. Robert Hughes, *American Visions*, BBC2 TV, 8 December 1996.

12. J. G. Ballard, 'One dull step for man . . .', *The Observer Review*, 22 December 1996, p. 15.

13. John Clute, *Science Fiction: the Illustrated Encyclopedia* (London, Dorling Kindersley, 1995), pp. 172–3.

14. Kingsley Amis, *New Maps of Hell: a Survey of Science Fiction* (London, Gollancz, 1961), p. 78.

15. Brian W. Aldiss, with David Wingrove, *Trillion Year Spree* (London, Gollancz, 1986), pp. 271f.

16. Ivor Rogers in Neil Barron, *Anatomy of Wonder: Science Fiction* (New York, Bowker, 1976), p. 88.

17. Miriam Allen de Ford, quoted in Brian W. Aldiss, *Billion Year Spree: the History of Science Fiction* (London, Corgi, 1973), p. 8.

18. Tom Shippey, ed., *Fictional Space: Essays on Contemporary Science Fiction* (Oxford, Blackwell, 1991), p. ix.

19. Thus Campbell, according to Aldiss, introduction to *Galactic Empires: II* (London, Futura, 1976), pp. vi–vii. The fact that humanity is 'an environment-changing animal' means that he can alter himself to the point of non self-recognition. Thus in Harry Harrison's story 'Final Encounter' (1964) a humanity searching for aliens among the stars believes it has discovered them, only to find they are humans who have gone around the galaxy 'the other way' and changed in the process. Here human plasticity is associated with the fabril mentality: both are typical of sf.

20. Shippey, *Fictional Space*, pp. ix, xiii.

21. John Clute and Peter Nicholls, eds., *The Encyclopedia of Science Fiction* (New York, St Martin's Press, 1993), p. 765.

Chapter 3 **The crucible of science fiction**

1. Mary Shelley, *Frankenstein*, ch. 5, beginning.

2. Brian W. Aldiss, *Billion Year Space: the History of Science Fiction*, (London, Corgi, 1973), p. 3.

3. John Clute, *Science Fiction: the Illustrated Encyclopedia* (London, Dorling Kindersley, 1995), p. 110.

4. Robert Scholes and Eric S. Rabkin, *Science Fiction: History, Science, Vision* (London, Oxford University Press, 1977), p. 193.

5. Aldiss, *Billion Year Spree*, p. 29.

6. Aldiss, *Billion Year Spree,* pp. 13, 29.

7. Karel Capek, the author of *R.U.R.* [Rossum's Universal Robots], (1920), the first robot story.

8. E.g., *Them!* (1954) – nuclear testing produces mutant giant ants – and *Conquest of Space* (1956).

9. *Daily Telegraph*, 20 September 1996, p. 8.

10. Karl Barth, *Dogmatics in Outline* tr. G. T. Thomson (London, SCM, 1966), p. 20.

11. Jürgen Moltmann, *Theology of Hope* (London, SCM, 1967), pp. 7, 23f.

12. Mark Rose, *Alien Encounters: Anatomy of Science Fiction.* Cambridge, Mass., Harvard University Press, 1981.

13. Ernst Fischer, *The Necessity of Art: a Marxist approach* (Harmondsworth: Penguin, 1963), p. 54, quoted in O. Edwards and G. Martin, *Romanticism* (Milton Keynes, Open University Press, 1972), p. 18. For 'The Wreck of the *Hope*', see plate 4 and

p. 56; on size, see pp. 54–5 on the paintings of John Martin.

14. H. R. Rookmaaker, *Modern Art and the Death of a Culture* (London, IVP, 1970), pp. 50f.

15. Whilst Terry Pratchett's Discworld novels make repeated references to a 'pluriverse', it is to be noted that he still has the Unseen *University*.

16. The sixth-century physicist John Philoponos queried many of Aristotle's assumptions, but was rejected by his own Christian Church (Harold Nebelsick, *Renaissance, Reformation and the Rise of Science*, Edinburgh, T. & T. Clark, 1992, pp. 11–18). Even Jacob Bronowski gives credit to Christianity for 'a different world of vision: not of abstract patterns, but of abounding and irrepressible life' (*The Ascent of Man*, London, Book Club Associates, 1977, p. 176). Cf. also Stanley Jaki, *Science and Creation* (Edinburgh, Scottish Academic Press, 1986), *The Saviour of Science* (Edinburgh, Scottish Academic Press, 1990); R. Hooykaas, *Religion and the Rise of Modern Science* (Grand Rapids, Mich., Eerdmans, 1978); T. F. Torrance, *Divine and Contingent Order* (Oxford, Oxford University Press, 1981); M. B. Foster, 'The Christian Doctrine of Creation and the Rise of Modern Science' (*Mind* 432, 1934, pp. 446–68).

17. Stephen Hawking, *A Brief History of Time* (London, Bantam, 1988), p. x.

18. Peter Atkins' article in John Cornwell, *Nature's Imagination: the Frontiers of Scientific Vision* (Oxford, Oxford University Press, 1995) is typically entitled 'The Limitless Power of Science' (pp. 122–32). Mary Midgley, 'Reductive Megalomania' in the same book is an excellent response (pp. 133–47); cf. also her *Science as Salvation: a Modern Myth and its Meaning*. London, Routledge, 1992.

19. Scholes and Rabkin, *Science Fiction*, p. 25.

20. Robert Silverberg in Neil Barron, *Anatomy of Wonder: Science Fiction* (New York, Bowker, 1976), p. 77.

21. Kingsley Amis, *New Maps of Hell: a Survey of Science Fiction* (London, Gollancz, 1961), pp. 37–9.

22. How come a computer virus developed by humans works on alien computers? Because they, like everyone else, have to use Bill Gates' Microsoft operating system!

23. Joanna Russ, quoted in Casey Fredericks, *The Future of Eternity: Mythologies of Science Fiction and Fantasy* (Bloomington, Ind., Indiana University Press, 1982), p. 115.

24. Michael Moorcock, quoting J. G. Ballard (Aldiss, *Billion Year Spree*, pp. 326–7).

25. 'H. G. Wells: Bromley Boy', BBC2 TV, 24 August 1996.

Chapter 4 **Mirror, mirror on the wall**

1. Quoted in Kingsley Amis, *New Maps of Hell: a Survey of Science Fiction* (London, Gollancz, 1961), p. 64.
2. Snow, in the film directed by Andrei Tarkovsky (1972), based on Stanislaw Lem's book (1961). Cf. Mark Rose, *Alien Encounters: Anatomy of Science Fiction* (Cambridge, Mass., Harvard University Press, 1981), pp. 82–95.
3. Darko Suvin, *Metamorphoses of Science Fiction: on the Poetics and History of a Literary Genre* (New Haven, Conn., Yale University Press, 1979), p. viii.
4. Quoting from Berthold Brecht's account of his concept of *Verfremdungseffekt* developed from the Marxist Formalist concept of *ostranenie* (Suvin, 'On the Poetics of the Science Fiction Genre' in Mark Rose, ed., *Science Fiction: a Collection of Critical Essays*, Englewood Cliffs, New Jersey, Prentice Hall, 1976, p. 60).
5. Quoted in Peter Nicholls, ed., *The Encyclopedia of Science Fiction: an Illustrated A to Z* (London, Granada, 1979), p. 160.
6. Darko Suvin in Rose, *Science Fiction*, pp. 59, 64.
7. David Hartwell, *Age of Wonders: Exploring the World of Science Fiction* (New York, Walker, 1984), p. 122. Chapter titles include: 'Worshipping at the Church of Wonder' and 'Let's get SF back in the gutter where it belongs'.
8. C. N. Manlove, *Christian Fantasy* (London, Macmillan, 1992), p. 2.
9. Nicholls, *Encyclopedia of Science Fiction*, p. 160, italics mine.
10. As feminist text, Radio Four arts discussion programme, September 1992; on Vietnam, Alasdair Spark, 'Vietnam: the War in science fiction', p. 124, in Philip J. Davies, ed., *Science Fiction: Social Conflict and War* (Manchester, Manchester University Press, 1990). Cf. also George E. Slusser and Eric S. Rabkin, eds., *Aliens: the Anthropology of Science Fiction* (Carbondale and Edwardsville, Ill., Southern Illinois University Press, 1987).
11. According to another model, sf moves from the known to the unknown: thus the title of a 1953 Pohl and Kornbluth classic, *The Space Merchants* (Amis, *New Maps of Hell*, p. 126). For Gary K. Wolfe (*The Known and the Unknown: Studies in the Iconology of Science Fiction*, Kent, Ohio, Kent State University Press, 1979), the genre is torn between the twin desires of making the unknown its own and rejoicing in its utter ineffability. David Ketterer (*New Worlds for Old: the Apocalyptic Imagination, Science Fiction and American Literature*, Bloomington, Ind., Indiana University Press, 1974), argues that in sf the known world must give way to another. Followed by many others like Frederick Kreuziger (*The Religion of Science Fiction*, Bowling Green, Ohio,

Bowling Green State University Popular Press, 1986), he compares sf with apocalyptic literature. Here another world comes into being catastrophically; in sf this happens too, even if only metaphorically 'in the reader's head' in a moment of conceptual breakthrough.

12. Amis, *New Maps of Hell*, pp. 94–5.

13. David Gerrold, *The World of Star Trek* (New York, Ballantine, 1973), pp. 32–4, 236; Susan Sackett, *Star Trek Speaks* (London, Futura, 1979), p. 101.

14. Brian W. Aldiss, *Billion Year Spree: the History of Science Fiction* (London, Corgi, 1973), pp. 122–3 n. 4, 132.

15. 'H. G. Wells: Bromley Boy', BBC2 TV, 24 August 1996.

16. Amis, *New Maps of Hell*, p. 95; Aldiss, *Billion Year Spree*, p. 366 n. 2; Ivor A. Rogers in Neil Barron, *Anatomy of Wonder: Science Fiction* (New York, Bowker, 1976), p. 95.

17. Christopher Priest in Patrick Parrinder, ed., *Science Fiction: a Critical Guide* (London, Longman, 1979), p. 195; Aldiss, *Billion Year Spree*, pp. 336–9.

18. C. N. Manlove, *Science Fiction: Ten Explorations* (London, Macmillan, 1986), p. 41.

19. John Clute, *Science Fiction: the Illustrated Encyclopedia* (London, Dorling Kindersley, 1995), p. 303.

20. Nicholls, *Encyclopedia of Science Fiction*, p. 473. Cf. also Peter Nicholls, ed., *The Science in Science Fiction* (London, Michael Joseph, 1982), pp. 200-1 ('Famous Bad Predictions').

21. Ursula K. Le Guin, *The Language of the Night: Essays on Fantasy and Science Fiction* (London, Women's Press, 1989), esp. pp. 135– 47. She wanted to give her revisionist *Earthsea* book, *Tehanu* (1989), the title *Better Late than Never!* (p. 45).

22. William Shatner, *Star Trek Memories* (London, HarperCollins, 1993), pp. 212–14. That he was right is proved by comments from Paul Boateng, Whoopi Goldberg and Mae Jemison.

23. David Brin, *Earth* (New York, Bantam, 1990), p. 584.

24. Thus Jack Williamson, *Wonder's Child: My Life in Science Fiction* (New York, Bluejay, 1984), p. 152.

25. Harlan Ellison, quoted by Frederick Pohl at a meeting of the Cambridge University Science Fiction Society, 16 October 1982.

Chapter 5 Enlightenment: disciples of the new religion

1. Stanislaw Lem, quoted in Edward James, *Science Fiction in the Twentieth Century* (Oxford: Oxford University Press, 1994), p. 144.

2. Ursula K. Le Guin, *The Language of the Night: Essays on Fantasy and Science Fiction* (London, Women's Press, 1989), pp. 90–1. The essay dates from 1976.

3. Kurt Vonnegut Jnr, *Wampeters, Foma & Granfalloms (Opinions)* (London, Jonathan Cape, 1975), pp. 29–33.

4. John Clute and Peter Nicholls, eds., *The Encyclopedia of Science Fiction* (New York, St Martin's Press, 1993), p. 1073; James, *Science Fiction*, pp. 143–5; James Gunn, ed., *The New Encyclopedia of Science Fiction* (New York, Viking Penguin, 1988), p. 273.

5. James, *Science Fiction*, ch. 4.

6. Stanislaw Lem, *Microworlds: Writing on Science Fiction and Fantasy* (London, Mandarin, 1991), p. 53. This is readily acknowledged by critics James Blish and Damon Knight.

7. Lem, *Microworlds*, p. 59.

8. Le Guin, *The Language of the Night*, pp. 87–8.

9. Larry Nemecek, *The Star Trek: The Next Generation Companion* (New York, Pocket, 1995), p. 143.

10. Scott Sanders in Patrick Parrinder, ed., *Science Fiction: a Critical Guide* (London, Longman, 1979), p. 133; Vonnegut, *Wampeters, Foma & Granfalloms*, 1975, pp. 29–30, 32.

11. C. S. Lewis, 'On Science Fiction' (1955) in *Of This and Other Worlds: Essays and Stories* (London, Collins, 1982), p. 87.

12. Le Guin, *The Language of the Night*, p. 90.

13. Patricia S. Warrick, *Mind in Motion: the Fiction of Philip K. Dick* (Carbondale and Edwardsville, Ill., Southern Illinois University Press, 1987), p. 120.

14. Douglas A. Mackey, *Philip K. Dick* (Boston, Mass., G. K. Hall, 1988), p. 90.

15. Brian W. Aldiss, *Trillion Year Spree* (London, Gollancz, 1986), p. 331.

16. Aldiss, *Trillion Year Spree*, p. 330.

17. Joseph E. Patrouch Jnr, *The Science Fiction of Isaac Asimov* (London, Denis Dobson, 1974), pp. 217–20.

18. Patrouch, *The Science Fiction of Isaac Asimov*, p. 261; Michael White, *Isaac Asimov: the Unauthorised Life* (London, Millennium, 1994), p. 208.

19. Clute and Nicholls, *Encyclopedia of Science Fiction*, p. 58.

20. The 1996 *Dr Who* TV film unsuccessfully turned the cerebral doctor into a Schwarzeneggerite 'Last Action Hero' in the hope of impressing American viewers.

21. Donald A. Wollheim, *The Universe Makers: Science Fiction Today*, (New York, Harper, 1971), pp. 6–7.

22. *Science Fiction Age* (21.1), p. 6.

23. Thus Leigh Brackett, *The Long Tomorrow* (1955); Piers Anthony, *Battle Circle* (1977); David Gemmell, *Wolf in Shadow* (1987).
24. Nemecek, *Next Generation Companion*, p. 14.
25. Greg Bear, *Tangents* (London, Gollancz, 1989), pp. 3–7.
26. Peter Nicholls, ed., *Science Fiction at Large* (London, Gollancz, 1976), p. 143.
27. Nicholls, *Science Fiction at Large*, pp. 152–3.

Chapter 6 Science and religion
part one: escape from religion

1. From Huxley's 1860 review of Darwin's *On the Origin of the Species*, in T. H. Huxley, *Collected Essays*, 9 vols. (London, Macmillan, 1893–4), II, pp. 52f, in the volume devoted to Darwiniana.
2. Richard Dawkins 'You are all alone in the Universe', book review of Carl Sagan and Ann Druyan's *Shadows of Forgotten Ancestors* in *The Observer*, 13 December 1992, p. 31.
3. Harry Harrison, *Captive Universe* (1970); Clifford Simak, 'Spacebred Generations' (1953); Brian Aldiss, *Non-Stop* (1958); Harlan Ellison, *The Starlost* (1973).
4. Robert Heinlein, 'Universe' (1941), in Groff Conklin, ed., *The Best of Science Fiction* (New York, Crown, 1946), p. 605.
5. George E. Slusser, *The Classic Years of Robert A. Heinlein* (San Bernardino, Calif., Borgo Press, 1977), p. 33.
6. James A. Blish, ed. Cy Chauvin, *The Tale that Wags The God* (Chicago, Advent, 1987), p. 3. 'Conceptual breakthrough' is also a major subtopic in David Ketterer, *Imprisoned in a Tesseract: the Life & Work of James Blish* (Kent, Ohio, Kent State University Press, 1987).
7. Kingsley Amis, *New Maps of Hell: a Survey of Science Fiction* (London, Gollancz, 1961), p. 83.
8. Philip José Farmer, *The Magic Labyrinth* (Frogmore, Panther, 1980), p. 17.
9. Alfred Bester, *Extro* (London, Methuen, 1976), p. 7.
10. Arthur C. Clarke, *The Fountains of Paradise* (London, Pan, 1979), p. 80.
11. E.g. Clifford Simak, *City* (London, Magnum, 1961), p. 161: 'religion, which had been losing ground for centuries, entirely disappeared'.
12. *Babylon 5*: 'And the Rock cried out, No Hiding Place', episode 3.20.
13. Several contributors to Robert Reilly, ed., *The Transcendent Adventure: Studies of Religion in Science Fiction/Fantasy* (Westport,

Conn., Greenwood Press, 1985) accuse the novel of the Manichean heresy.

14. In Dan Simmons, *Endymion* (1996), we learn how the cruciform later becomes the basis for a renovated Catholicism that is truly the work of an Antichrist.

15. Alexander Butyrm of some Asimov characters in Reilly, *The Transcendent Adventure*, p. 61.

16. H. G. Wells, 'The Grisly Folk' (1896) and 'A Tale of the Stone Age' (1897); Arthur C. Clarke, *2001: A Space Odyssey*.

17. *Star Trek: The Original Series*, 'The Paradise Syndrome' and *Star Trek: The Next Generation*, 'The Chase'. Brian Aldiss gives an introduction to the theme in *Galactic Empires: II* (London, Weidenfeld and Nicholson, 1976).

18. Casey Fredericks, *The Future of Eternity: Mythologies of Science Fiction and Fantasy* (Bloomington, Ind., Indiana State University Press, 1982), p. 8.

19. Peter Nicholls and John Brosnan in John Clute and Peter Nicholls, eds., *The Encyclopedia of Science Fiction* (New York, St Martin's Press, 1993), p. 1219.

Chapter 7 **Science and religion part two: eggheads and energy**

1. Peter Brown, *The World of Late Antiquity* (London: Thames and Hudson, 1971), p. 80.

2. Brian W. Aldiss, *Billion Year Spree: the History of Science Fiction* (London, Corgi, 1973), p. 331 n.

3. Peter Brown, *Augustine of Hippo* (London, Faber, 1967), pp. 46–60 applies these categories to Manichaeism, but they are equally applicable to Gnosticism itself.

4. Thus David Halperin, 'Gnosticism in High Tech: Science Fiction and Cult Formation' in D. Halperin, ed., *Psychodynamic Perspectives on Religion, Sect and Cult* (Boston, Mass., John Wright PGSC Inc., 1983), pp. 257–66; Douglas A. Mackey, 'Science Fiction and Gnosticism' (*Missouri Review* 7.2, February 1984, pp. 112–20); Robert Galbreath, 'Fantastic Literature as Gnosis' (*Extrapolation* 29.4, Winter 1988, pp. 330–7).

5. Alfred Bester, *The Demolished Man* (1953), published in Damon Knight, ed., *A Science Fiction Argosy* (London, Gollancz, 1973), p. 434.

6. John Clute and Peter Nicholls, eds., *The Encyclopedia of Science Fiction* (New York, St Martin's Press, 1993), p. 593. A number of Hollywood film stars (Tom Cruise, Nicole Kidman, John Travolta)

are enthusiastic supporters of Scientology, the latter's 1996 film *Phenomenon* being a subtle piece of propaganda for the cult's ideals.

7. Quoted in John J. Pierce, *Great Themes of Science Fiction, a Study in Imagination and Evolution* (New York, Greenwood Press, 1987), p. 31.

8. Frederick Pohl and Cyril Kornbluth, *Wolfbane* (London, Gollancz, 1986), p. 189.

9. Douglas Robillard, 'Uncertain Futures: Damon Knight's sf' in Thomas D. Clareson, ed., *Voices for thr Future*, vol. III (Bowling Green, Ohio, Bowling Green University Popular Press, 1984), pp. 30–51, here p. 8.

10. There are many other examples of the same sort of thing: Fredrick Pohl's classic short story 'Day Million' (1966), Harry Harrison's 'Final Encounter' (1964), Philip Mann's *Pioneers* (1988), James Blish's *The Seedling Stars* (1957).

11. Greg Bear, *Anvil of Stars* (London, Century, 1992), p. 89. Cf. also *Star Trek: The Next Generation*: 'Lonely among us' (episode 108), 'Where No One has Gone Before' (episode 106) and 'Transfigurations' (episode 173), among many others.

12. Arthur C. Clarke, *2001: A Space Odyssey* (London, Arrow, 1968), pp. 251–6.

13. C. N. Manlove, *Science Fiction: Ten Explorations* (London, Macmillan, 1986), p. 5.

14. Algis Budrys, *Rogue Moon* (1960), quoted in Pringle, 1985, p. 84.

15. *The Best of A. E. Van Vogt, Vol. II* (London, Sphere, 1984), p. 200.

16. See particularly Julian May's *Jack the Bodiless* (1992) and *Diamond Mask* (1994).

17. John Clute, *Science Fiction: the Illustrated Encyclopedia* (London, Dorling Kindersley, 1995), p. 89. So too Frank J. Tipler's notorious *Modern Cosmology, God and the Resurrection of the Dead* (New York, Doubleday, 1994). Here it is argued that within 10 billion billion years humanity will have expanded through the universe and be able to harness the energy of its contraction to perfectly simulate within computers every creature that ever existed, or ever could exist. Since this finite time will subjectively feel like eternity, and each of us will have the best possible world created for us, we can call this Resurrection. George Johnson, a reviewer in the *New York Times*, like many others found this book simultaneously mind-boggling and incredible.

18. P. Teilhard de Chardin, *Human Energy*, tr. J. M. Cohen (London, Collins, 1969), p. 52.

19. Donald G. Bloesch, *God the Almighty: Power, Wisdom, Holiness, Love* (Downers Grove, Ill., IVP, 1995), p. 245. Bloesch's argument

finds weight from Susan A. Anderson's sympathetic study, 'Evolutionary Futurism in Stapledon's "Star Maker"' (*Process Studies*, vol. 5, Summer 1975, pp. 123–8).

20. In turn: Brian Stableford, *Scientific Romance in Britain*, 1890–1950 (London, Fourth Estate, 1985); Clute, *Science Fiction: the Illustrated Encyclopedia*, p. 122; Aldiss, *Billion Year Spree*, p. 236.

21. Aldiss, *Billion Year Spree*, p. 229.

22. Brian Aldiss, introduction to Olaf Stapledon, *Last and First Men* (Harmondsworth, Penguin, 1938, orig. 1930), pp. 6–10.

23. Aldiss, in Stapledon, *Last and First Men*, p. 9.

24. Aldiss, in Stapledon, *Last and First Men*, p. 7.

25. Aldiss, in Stapledon, *Last and First Men*, p. 10.

26. Robert Scholes and Eric S. Rabkin, *Science Fiction: History, Science, Vision* (London, Oxford University Press, 1977), p. 212.

27. Curtis C. Smith, 'Olaf Stapledon's Dispassionate Objectivity' in Clareson, *Voices for the Future*, vol. I (1976), pp. 44–63.

28. Stapledon, *Last and First Men*, p. 288.

29. Gary K. Wolfe, ed., *Science Fiction Dialogues* (Chicago, Academy, 1982).

30. Aldiss, *Billion Year Spree*, p. 235.

31. Smith, in Clareson, *Voices for the Future*, vol. I (1976), p. 45.

32. Galbreath, 'Fantastic Literature as Gnosis', pp. 332, 334.

33. E.g., *Palace of Eternity* (1983); *Orbitsville Departure* (1985); *The Wooden Spaceships* (1988).

34. Also through Dick's transparent affinity to cultish paranoia. Dick's theories are tragically reminiscent of another California group – the 'Heaven's Gate' cult who committed mass suicide in March 1997, in expectation of a ride to heaven on a UFO travelling with the comet Hale-Bopp.

35. Mackey, 'Science Fiction and Gnosticism', pp. 117, 119.

36. Cf. also John Rothfork, 'Science Fiction as a Religious Guide to the New Age' (*Kansas Quarterly* 10, Fall 1978, pp. 57–66, esp. pp. 58–62).

Chapter 8 **The divinity of creation**

1. Ben Bova (*OMNI* 2.4, January 1980, p. 6).

2. I.e., he invented them in order to show the inherent moral weakness of 'gods' in general. The list is endless: 'Adonis, V'ger, Charlie X, the Squire of Gothos, Nomad and Q, just to reprise a mere half-dozen of the Deity-as-Demento that Roddenberry either wrote himself or forced into the work of others' (Harlan Ellison, *The City on the Edge of Forever*, Clarkston, Ga., White Wolf, 1996, pp. 24–5).

3. James Michener (*OMNI* 3.7, April 1981, pp. 48–9 and 102–4).

4. Thomas D. Clareson, ed., *Voices for the Future*, vol. I (Bowling Green, Ohio, Bowling Green University Popular Press, 1976), pp. 217–90.

5. Ben Bova, *Mars* (1992); Frederick Pohl, *Mining the Oort* (1992); Kim Stanley Robinson, *Red Mars* (1992) and successors; Greg Bear, *Moving Mars* (1993); Paul McAuley, *Red Dust* (1993).

6. Media reaction to NASA's announcement moved away from initial hysteria to growing caution. The meteorite led to a Clinton press conference, Patrick Moore on the *News at Ten*, instant TV documentaries, *Newsweek and Time* covers, and so forth. NASA has a vested interest in mission funding.

7. The opinions of Doug Beason, Robert Zubrin and Geoffrey Landis (*Science Fiction Age*, May 1993, pp. 26–9). Cf. also Zubrin, *The Case for Mars* (New York, Simon and Schuster, 1996).

8. Thus Gordon R. Dickson, 'Danger – Human' (1958). In 1961, Kingsley Amis commented that: 'it is almost obligatory that when Galactic Headquarters get the news that space-ships have been detected leaving Sol III, everybody should hold up his tentacles in astonishment: "Impossible!" Vora will say; "they've only had the internal combustion engine for a century or so"' (Kingsley Amis, *New Maps of Hell: a Survey of Science Fiction*, London, Gollancz, 1961, p. 79).

9. Malcolm Edwards in Peter Nicholls, *The Encyclopedia of Science Fiction: an Illustrated A to Z* (London, Granada, 1979), pp. 511, 312.

10. John Clute in Nicholls, *Encyclopedia*, p. 32.

11. C. S. Lewis, *Out of the Silent Planet* (London, Pan, 1952), pp. 157–60.

12. C. S. Lewis, 'Religion and Rocketry' (1958) in W. Hooper, ed., *Fern-seed and Elephants* (Glasgow, Collins, 1975), p. 91. Cf. also Brian Aldiss, *Billion Year Spree: the History of Science Fiction* (London, Corgi, 1973), p. 224. The origin of this story lies in H. G. Wells' *First Men in the Moon*, and the Selenite Grand Lunar's hearing of Cavor.

13. Robert Heinlein, *Have Spacesuit, Will Travel* (1958), quoted in George E. Slusser, *The Classic Years of Robert A. Heinlein* (San Bernardino, Calif., Borgo Press, 1977), p. 57.

14. Heinlein, *Have Spacesuit, Will Travel*, quoted in Donald A. Wollheim, *The Universe Makers: Science Fiction Today* (New York, Harper, 1971), p. 102.

15. Wollheim, *The Universe Makers*, p. 102.

16. Wollheim, *The Universe Makers*, p. 118.

17. Wollheim, *The Universe Makers*, p. 99.

18. Stephen R. L. Clark, *How to Live Forever: Science Fiction and Philosophy* (London, Routledge, 1995), p. 5.

19. Standard sf treatments are Robert Heinlein's *The Door into Summer* (1957) and *Methuselah's Children* (1958).

20. E.g., Neil Barron, *Anatomy of Wonder: Science Fiction* (New York, Bowker, 1976), p. 151.

21. Cf. also the *Star Trek: The Next Generation* episode, 'Relics' (episode 230). A Dyson sphere is an artificial biosphere completely enclosing its sun. It is based on the hypothesis that a civilization is limited by the energy available to it; it or a ringworld (an engineering compromise, a vast continuous constructed planetary ring) would provide for vastly more energy and space.

22. Joe Haldeman, *The Long Habit of Living* (1989).

23. Stanley Jaki, *Cosmos and Creator* (Edinburgh, Scottish Academic Press, 1980), p. 21, p. 145 n. 42.

24. Stanley Jaki, *Science and Creation* (Edinburgh, Scottish Academic Press, 1986).

25. Steven Weinberg, *The First Three Minutes* (Glasgow, Collins, 1978), p. 148.

26. Thus Herodotus and Thucydides. Cf. Samuel Sambursky, *The Physical Science of Late Antiquity* (London, RKP, 1962).

27. Wollheim, *The Universe Makers*, p. 48.

28. Colin Russell, *Cross-Currents* (Leicester, IVP, 1985), pp. 49–53.

29. Michael R. Collings, *Brian Aldiss* (Washington, Starmont House, 1986), p. 75.

30. Carl D. Malmgren, *Worlds Apart: Narratology of Science Fiction* (Bloomington, Ind., Indiana University Press, 1991), p. 132. As he points out (p. 138) in books like *The Drowned World* (1962) 'we experience the radical submission of Self to World'.

31. Cf. Brian W. Aldiss, *Science Fiction Art: the Fantasies of SF* (London, NEL, 1975) for sundry examples; also Harry Harrison, *Great Balls of Fire! A History of Sex in Science Fiction* (Grosset and Dunlap, 1977).

32. Erich von Däniken above all (e.g., *Chariots of the Gods*, 1969).

33. Cf. Robert Heinlein's predestinarian *The Puppet Masters* (1951); Eric Frank Russell's *Three to Conquer* (1955) and particularly (among many others) the film *Invaders from Mars* (1953); also the 'Conspiracy' episode of *Star Trek: The Next Generation* (episode 125).

34. For a sceptical response, see Patrick Parrinder, ed., *Science Fiction: a Critical Guide* (London, Longman, 1979), p. 157. Ivan Yefremov's Marxist reply, 'Cor Serpentis' (1959) blamed the problem on capitalist aggressiveness!

35. Murray McLachlan in John Clute and Peter Nicholls, eds., *The*

Encyclopedia of Science Fiction (New York, St Martin's Press, 1993), p. 774.

36. John J. Pierce, *Great Themes of Science Fiction: a Study in Imagination and Evolution* (New York, Greenwood Press, 1987), p. 21.
37. Amis, *New Maps of Hell*, p. 84.
38. Amis, *New Maps of Hell*, p. 82.
39. John Griffiths, *Three Tomorrows: American, British and Soviet Science Fiction* (London, Macmillan, 1980), p. 156.
40. Cf. Walter Sullivan, *We Are Not Alone* (Harmondsworth, Penguin, 1964; rev. edn. 1970).
41. Nicholls, *Encyclopedia*, p. 122.
42. At the end of the second *Star Trek* film (*Revenge of Khan*, 1982).
43. Tom Woodman, 'Science fiction, religion and transcendence' in Parrinder, *Science Fiction*, p. 121.

Chapter 9 **A lonely universe**

1. Michael Swanwick, *Vacuum Flowers* (London, Simon and Schuster, 1987), p. 1.
2. Swanwick, *Vacuum Flowers*, p. 99.
3. Eric Frank Russell's 'Gandhism' of '. . . And then there were None' (1951) is an exception.
4. Leon Stover, *Robert A. Heinlein* (Boston, Mass., G. K. Hall, 1987), p. 47.
5. Alexei Panshin, quoted in Brian W. Aldiss, *Billion Year Spree: the History of Science Fiction* (London, Corgi, 1973), p. 309.
6. Robert Scholes and Eric S. Rabkin, *Science Fiction: History, Science, Vision* (London, Oxford University Press, 1967), pp. 56–7. Heinlein is, strictly speaking, a libertarian; he was heavily influenced by the 'objectivist' philosophy of Ayn Rand (*Anthem*, 1946; *Atlas Shrugged*, 1957), and is in company with other sf writers like Poul Anderson and Jerry Pournelle.
7. This book has been blamed for contributing to Charles Manson's murder of Sharon Tate – thus Aldiss, *Billion Year Spree*, pp. 212–3, but angrily refuted by Stover, *Robert A. Heinlein*.
8. John Sladek, in the brilliant parodies to be found in *The Steam-Driven Boy and Other Strangers* (1973).
9. Peter Nicholls, ed., *The Encyclopedia of Science Fiction: an Illustrated A to Z* (London, Granada, 1979), p. 554; J. A. Sutherland in Patrick Parrinder, ed., *Science Fiction: a Critical Guide* (London, Longman, 1979), p. 170.
10. Jack Williamson, *Wonder's Child: my Life in Science Fiction* (New York, Bluejay, 1984), pp. 122–3.

11. Kingsley Amis, *New Maps of Hell: a Survey of Science Fiction* (London, Gollancz, 1961), p. 79.
12. Søren Kierkegaard, *Concluding Unscientific Postscript*, tr. David F. Swenson and Walter Lowrie (Princeton, Princeton University Press, 1968), p. 224. Cf. also A. Heron, *A Century of Protestant Theology* (Guildford, Lutterworth, 1980), pp. 47–51.
13. John MacMurray, *The Self as Agent* (London, Faber, 1969); *Persons in Relation* (New York, Harper, 1961).
14. Although the Greek word *atomos* meant 'indivisible unit', atoms in reality are very interrelational. Harold Turner has suggested 'marbles' as a replacement, so long as we remember there is no bag to hold the marbles together!
15. Colin Gunton, 'The One, the Three and the Many', King's College London Inaugural Lecture, 1985, p. 6, reprinted in Gunton, *The Promise of Trinitarian Theology* (Edinburgh, T. & T. Clark, 1991, 2nd edn 1997). Cf. also T. F. Torrance, *Theological Science* (London, Oxford University Press 1969; reissued Edinburgh, T. & T. Clark 1996), pp. 305–7; J. Moltmann, *The Trinity and the Kingdom of God* (London, SCM, 1981).
16. Cf. BCC Report and Study Guide, *The Forgotten Trinity* (London, 1989); also J. Zizioulas, *Being as Communion* (London, Darton, Longman and Todd, 1985) and Catherine Mowry LaCugna, *God for Us* (New York, HarperCollins, 1991), pp. 243–305 – among others.
17. The cases are not identical, since God is different from us; nevertheless, God's existence as a loving communion in whom the persons of the Trinity exist in and for one another is the model of existence for the Church and indeed all creatures.
18. John Zizioulas, 'Human Capacity and Human Incapacity: A Theological Exploration of Personhood' (*Scottish Journal of Theology* 28, 1975, pp. 401–48).
19. Karl Barth, *Church Dogmatics, Vol. IV.2*, tr. G. W. Bromiley (Edinburgh: T. & T. Clark, 1958), p. 185.

Chapter 10 Between two worlds: science fiction and postmodernism

1. Kim Stanley Robinson (*Mississippi Review*, 1988) quoted in David Ketterer, *Canadian Science Fiction and Fantasy* (Bloomington, Ind., Indiana University Press, 1992), p. 141. Of the many other writers in this area, Bruce Sterling is the other outstanding one. Walter Jon Williams' *Voice of the Whirlwind* (1987) may be mentioned as typical of the subgenre: a corporatist

future, tailored viruses, orbiting cities, addiction, cloning. William Gibson's own *Burning Chrome* (1986), a collection of short stories, and *Neuromancer* successors, *Count Zero* (1986) and *Mona Lisa Overdrive* (1988) are as punchy, fast-paced and well-written as *Neuromancer*. A violent film version of one story emerged as *Johnny Mnemonic* (1996).

2. John Clute, *Science Fiction: the Illustrated Encyclopedia* (London, Dorling Kindersley, 1995), p. 89.

3. Gibson's writing is characterized by a 'relentlessly hip bravura documentation of the accoutrements, the semiotic fragments of a retro-future': Ketterer, *Canadian Science Fiction and Fantasy*, pp. 143–4.

4. For a wickedly entertaining parody, see Harry Harrison's 'Cy BerPunk's Tale' in his *The Galactic Hero on the Planet of Robot Slaves* (1989).

5. Ketterer, *Canadian Science Fiction and Fantasy*, p. 143.

6. Tom Shippey, ed., *Fictional Space: Essays on Contemporary Science Fiction* (Oxford, Basil Blackwell, 1991), pp. 2, 31 n. 2; cf. also Clute, *Encyclopedia*, p. 232.

7. John Clute and Peter Nicholls, eds., *The Encyclopedia of Science Fiction* (New York, St Martin's Press, 1993), pp. 495–6.

8. Clute, *Encyclopedia*, p. 88.

9. Clute, *Encyclopedia*, p. 199.

10. William Gibson, *Neuromancer* (London, Grafton, 1984), p. 52.

11. Gibson, *Neuromancer*, p. 12 (cf. also pp. 181, 285).

12. Clute, *Encyclopedia*, p. 89.

13. Ketterer, *Canadian Science Fiction and Fantasy*, p. 143.

14. Clute and Nicholls, *Encyclopedia*, p. 148.

15. David Attenborough, as President of the British Scientific Association (*Daily Telegraph*, 24 August 1992, p. 11).

16. Thus, 'the natural world is just an inert resource we can conquer and use if we like'; 'the universe is fields of force governed by laws of nature' (*The Real Thing*, Channel 4 TV series, August 1992).

17. The modernist dream already began to be exploded by Einsteinian relativity and quantum mechanics. Chaos theory is interpreted as knocking an extra nail in the coffin. It says that certain non-equilibrium systems are inherently unpredictable and hence – by extension – uncontrollable. *Jurassic Park* acts for Crichton as a gigantic workshop to prove the truth of his hypothesis.

18. This makes the apparently merely humorous ditty in the film significant – GRANT: 'God creates dinosaurs; God destroys dinosaurs; God creates man; Man creates dinosaurs . . .' SADLER: '. . . Dinosaurs eat man; Woman inherits the earth.' In

other words, male attitudes have brought about the danger; female ones are needed for salvation.

19. Peter Nicholls, ed., *The Encyclopedia of Science Fiction: an Illustrated A to Z* (London, Granada, 1979), pp. 15–16.

20. Thus Patricia S. Warrick, *Mind in Motion: the Fiction of Philip K. Dick* (Carbondale and Edwardsville, Ill., Southern Illinois University Press, 1987), pp. 21–5, who interprets quantum mechanics as implying 'that all laws are creations of the human mind' (p. 24); also A. Goswami with M. Goswami, *The Cosmic Dancers: Exploring the Physics of Science Fiction*. New York, Harper and Row, 1983.

21. Douglas Adams, *The Restaurant at the End of the Universe* (1980), p. 184.

22. Adams, *The Restaurant at the End of the Universe,* pp. 59, 64.

23. Thus, in Richard Dawkins' aforementioned review ('You are all alone in the Universe' in *The Observer*, 13 December 1992, p. 31), he takes great delight in the uncongenial 'cold truths of our scientific age', which imply precisely that 'the world was not made for us'. Cf. by contrast Stanley Jaki, *Cosmos and Creator* (Edinburgh, Scottish Academic Press, 1980), ch. 5. 'A trap or a home?'!

24. Stanley Jaki, *The Saviour of Science.* Edinburgh, Scottish Academic Press, 1990.

Chapter 11 **Conclusion: a new foundation**

1. Ursula K. Le Guin, *Planet of Exile* (London, Star, 1983), p. 196.

2. J. Moltmann, 'What is "New" in Christianity: the Category *Novum* in Christian Theology', in *Religion, Revolution and the Future* tr. M. D. Meeks (New York, Scribner, 1969), pp. 3–4.

3. J. R. R. Tolkien, *The Return of the King* (London, George Allen and Unwin, 1955), p. 199.

4. Kim Stanley Robinson's *Red Mars* (1992) raises the interesting question of the ethics of terraforming. Although, in his book, 'Christians' are in favour of ruthless exploitation (as well as corruption, murder *and* fuzzy thinking), I would argue – as an actual Christian – that if God is the creator of all, it is highly dubious whether humans have the right to turn other worlds into carbon-copies of our own, simply because we prefer it that way. C. S. Lewis would not think so either.

5. Ursula K. Le Guin, *The Dispossessed* (Frogmore, Panther, 1976), p. 131. Some sf authors have shared a repeated fascination for animals, particularly the dog (Fredric Brown, 'Search', 1954;

Clifford Simak, *City*, 1961; Eric Frank Russell, 'Follower', 1957). This is perhaps because in its apparent devotion to humans it can act as a metaphor for another form of worship.

6. Julian May, *The Adversary* (London, Pan, 1984), p. 84.
7. John Clute and Peter Nicholls, eds., *The Encyclopedia of Science Fiction* (New York, St Martin's Press, 1993), p. 703.
8. Le Guin, *Planet of Exile*, p. 238.
9. Le Guin, *The Dispossessed*, p. 266.
10. Jeremy Pascal, *The Movies from 1930 to the Present* (London, Hamlyn, 1984), p. 282.
11. Karl Barth, *Church Dogmatics, Vol. IV.1*, tr. G. W. Bromiley (Edinburgh: T. & T. Clark, 1956), p. 186, where he criticizes it for seeming to assume a prior knowledge that God is other than us. If so, God is in fact encompassed in our own understanding after all (for we already know he is different from us!). The only real knowledge of otherness can be by a revelation from beyond ourselves, which simultaneously accommodates our minds to understand it.
12. T. F. Torrance, *Theology in Reconstruction* (London, SCM, 1965), pp. 48–9.
13. T. F. Torrance, 'St. Paul and Athenagoras at Athens' (*Scottish Journal of Theology*, 41.1, 1988, pp. 11–26).
14. John Calvin, *Institute* I.1.
15. Moltmann, 'What is "New" in Christianity'.
16. Quoted to me in a personal conversation by John Thompson. Cf. E. Jüngel, *The Doctrine of the Trinity: God's Being is in Becoming* (Edinburgh, Scottish Academic Press, 1976).
17. Arthur C. Clarke, *Rama Revealed* (London, Gollancz, 1993), p. 477.
18. John Clute, *Science Fiction: the Illustrated Encyclopedia* (London, Dorling Kindersley, 1995), p. 122.
19. Thus too the horrific classic, 'It's a *good* life' by Jerome Bixby (1953), wherein a psychically gifted child rules the lives of others by whim.
20. David Mogen, *Ray Bradbury* (Boston, Mass., G. K. Hall, 1986), p. 63.
21. Willis McNelly, 1969, quoted in Mogen, *Ray Bradbury*, p. 64.
22. Quoted in Mogen, *Ray Bradbury*, pp. 82, 93.
23. Quoted in Mogen, *Ray Bradbury*, pp. 68-9.
24. Joni Mitchell, 'Woodstock' ('Ladies of the Canyon', record album, Reprise, 1970).
25. A recent cartoon in *Newsweek* showed a Martian colonist reading a newspaper with flying saucers in the background: the lead article of the paper was 'West Bank violence on Earth continues'.

26. Peter Nicholls, ed., *The Science in Science Fiction* (London, Michael Joseph, 1982), p. 106.

27. Relativistic projectiles like these are used in Vernor Vinge's *A Fire upon the Deep* (1992) with devastating effect. A less violent one was used in the *Dr Who* story 'Earthshock'. In Larry Niven and Jerry Pournelle's *Footfall* (1985) an asteroid is deliberately dropped by aliens upon the Indian Ocean, swamping most of Africa and the Indian subcontinent and drowning their inhabitants; the authors seem to think this an appropriate revenge on OPEC.

28. Very few futures found in science fiction show destruction of even this scale. Normally they remain at the level of spaceships annihilating one another in battle, itself a highly improbable scenario due to the relativistic velocities involved (for an even weirder one, see Niven's *Protector*, 1973). The model used is of mercenary wars à la Pournelle, or *Star Trek*-like Napoleonic naval engagements that barely touch civilians apart from outposts – in other words, very like C. S. Forester, on whose creation of Horatio Hornblower Kirk was modelled. To have ships blasting away at one another in virtually stationary positions is an utterly anachronistic scenario and not even accurate now.

Further reading

There is so much sf criticism now that it is impossible to read all of it, let alone survey all the new fiction and films. I do not include all I have read below. Asterisks indicate particularly recommended works. Please see the bibliographies in Barron, James, Malmgren and Reilly for more suggestions. James and Clute particularly provide useful suggestions for reading.

Recommended general reference works:

*Clute, John, *Science Fiction: the Illustrated Encyclopedia* (London, Dorling Kindersley, 1995) is opionated, up to date, beautifully written and superbly illustrated; an excellent introduction to sf criticism.

*Aldiss, Brian W., *Billion Year Spree: the History of Science Fiction* (London, Corgi, 1973) is an excellent introductory work. Aldiss, Brian W., with David Wingrove, *Trillion Year Spree* (London, Gollancz, 1986) is updated but rather wordy.

*Nicholls, Peter, ed., *The Encyclopedia of Science Fiction: an Illustrated A to Z* (London, Granada, 1979) became the essential 'Bible' for sf reference.
*Clute, John and Nicholls, Peter, eds., *The Encyclopedia of Science Fiction* (New York, St Martin's Press, 1993), has lost the illustrations of the original and become thicker, heavier and hardback. It is still essential.
*Fulton, Roger, *The Encyclopedia of TV Science Fiction* (London, Boxtree/TV Times, 1995) is very up to date and invaluable. It includes all US TV shows shown in the UK.
Hardy, Phil, ed., *The Aurum Film Encyclopedia: Science Fiction* (London, Aurum Press, 1995) is comprehensive, if occasionally rather tendentious.

*Barron, Neil, *Anatomy of Wonder: Science Fiction* (New York; Bowker,

1976) is a very good annotated bibliography of fictional and critical works. There are more recent versions.

Pringle, David, *The Ultimate Guide to Science Fiction* (London, Grafton, 1990) gives brief summaries of some 3000 sf novels, rated in numbers of asterisks, whilst his *Science Fiction: the 100 Best Novels* (London, Xanadu, 1985) leaves lots of room for argument, which is, of course, half the fun.

Other useful reference works are:

Fletcher, Marilyn P., ed., *Reader's Guide to the Twentieth Century.* Chicago, American Library Association, 1989.

Gunn, James, ed., *The New Encyclopedia of Science Fiction.* New York, Viking Penguin, 1988.

*Holdstock, Robert, ed., *The Encyclopedia of Science Fiction.* London, Octopus, 1978.

Gunden, Kenneth von, *Flights of Fancy: the Great Fantasy Films.* Jefferson, North Car., McFarland, 1989.

Post, J. B., comp., *An Atlas of Fantasy.* London, Saviour, 1979.

Renard, J.-B., 'Religion, Science-Fiction et Extraterrestres: De la littérature à la croyance' *(Archives de Sciences Sociales des Religions,* 50.(1), Juillet–Septembre, 1980).

Searles, B., Last, M., Meacham, B. and Franklin, M., *A Reader's Guide to Science Fiction.* New York, Facts on File, 1980.

Variety, *Science Fiction Movies.* London, Hamlyn, 1992.

Wingrove, David, ed., *The Source Book of Science Fiction.* New York, Van Nostrand Reinhold, 1984.

General bibliography

Aldiss, Brian W., *Bury My Heart at W. H. Smith's.* London, Hodder and Stoughton, 1990.

*Aldiss, Brian W., *Science Fiction Art: the Fantasies of SF.* London, NEL, 1975.

Aldiss, Brian W. and Harrison, Harry, eds., *Farewell, Fantastic Venus: a History of the Planet Venus in Fact and Fiction.* London, Macdonald, 1968.

Aldiss, Brian W. and Harrison, Harry, eds., *Hell's Cartographers: Some Personal Histories of Science Fiction Writers.* London, Weidenfeld and Nicolson, 1975.

Allan, John, *The Gospel according to Science Fiction.* London, Falcon, 1975.

Allen, Dick, *Science Fiction: The Future.* New York, Harcourt Brace Jovanovitch, 1971.

*Amis, Kingsley, *New Maps of Hell: a Survey of Science Fiction*. London, Gollancz, 1961.

Anderson, Susan A., 'Evolutionary Futurism in Stapledon's "Star Maker"', (*Process Studies* 5, Summer 1975, pp. 123–8).

Asherman, Allan, *The Star Trek Compendium*. London, Titan, 1989.

Asimov, Isaac, *Asimov on Science Fiction*. New York, Doubleday, 1981.

Asimov, Isaac, *Asimov's Galaxy: Reflections on Science Fiction*. New York, Doubleday, 1989.

Bainbridge, William Sims, *Dimensions of Science Fiction*. Cambridge, Mass., Harvard University Press, 1986.

Barr, Marlene S., *Alien to Femininity: Speculative Fiction and Feminist Theory*. New York, Greenwood Press, 1987.

Bassom, David, *Creating Babylon 5*. London, Boxtree, 1996.

Bittner, James W., *Approaches to the Fiction of Ursula K. Le Guin*. Michigan, UMI Research Press, 1984.

Blair, Karin, 'Sex and *Star Trek*' (*Science Fiction Studies* 10, November 1983, pp. 292–7).

Blish, James, ed. Cy Chauvin, *The Tale That Wags The God*. Chicago, Advent, 1987.

Bretnor, Reginald A., *Science Fiction, Today and Tomorrow*. New York, Harper and Row, 1974.

Casey, John, ed., *William Golding: the Man and his Books*. London, Faber, 1986.

*Clareson, Thomas D., ed., *The Other Side of Realism*. Bowling Green, Ohio, Bowling Green University Popular Press, 1971.

*Clareson, Thomas D., ed., *Voices for the Future*, vol. I–III. Bowling Green, Ohio, Bowling Green University Popular Press, 1976, 1979, 1984.

Clark, Stephen R. L., *How to Live Forever: Science Fiction and Philosophy*. London, Routledge, 1995.

Clarke, I. F., *Voices Prophesying War: Future Wars, 1763–3749*. Oxford, Oxford University Press, 1992.

Collings, Michael R., *Brian Aldiss*. Washington, Starmont House, 1986.

Cranny-Francis, Anne, 'Sexuality and Sexual Stereotyping in *Star Trek*' (*Science Fiction Studies* 12, November 1985, pp. 274–84).

Davenport, Basil, *The Science Fiction Novel: Imagination and Social Criticism*. Chicago, Advent, 1964.

Davies, Philip J., ed., *Science Fiction: Social Conflict and War*. Manchester, Manchester University Press, 1990.

Dowling, David, *Fictions of Nuclear Disaster*. London, 1987.

Dozois, Garner R. and Dann, Jack A., eds., *Aliens!* New York, Pocket, 1980.

Edwards, Malcolm and Holdstock, Robert, *Realms of Fantasy.* Limpsfield, Dragon's World, 1983.

Ellison, Harlan, *The City on the Edge of Forever.* Clarkston, Ga.: White Wolf, 1996.

Franklin, H. Bruce, *Robert A. Heinlein: America as Science Fiction.* Oxford: Oxford University Press, 1980.

Fredericks, Casey, *The Future of Eternity: Mythologies of Science Fiction and Fantasy.* Bloomington, Ind., Indiana University Press, 1982.

Galbreath, Robert, 'Fantastic Literature as Gnosis' (*Extrapolation*, 29.4, Winter 1988, pp. 330–7).

Garnett, Rhys and Ellis, R. J., *Science Fiction: Roots and Branches.* Houndmills, Basingstoke, Macmillan, 1990.

Gerrold, David, *The World of Star Trek.* New York, Ballantine, 1973.

Goswami A. with Goswami M., *The Cosmic Dancers: Exploring the Physics of Science Fiction.* New York, Harper and Row, 1983.

Greenland, C., Rabkin, E. S. and Slusser, G. E., *Storm Warnings: Science Fiction Confronts the Future.* Carbondale and Edwardsville, Ill., Southern Illinois University Press, 1987.

Griffiths, John, *Three Tomorrows: American, British and Soviet Science Fiction.* London, Macmillan, 1980.

Gunn, James, *Alternative Worlds.* New Jersey, Prentice-Hall, 1975.

Gunn, James, *Isaac Asimov: The Foundations of Science Fiction.* New York, Oxford University Press, 1982.

Haining, Peter, *The Dr Who File.* London, W. H. Allen, 1986.

Halperin, David, 'Gnosticism in High Tech: Science Fiction and Cult Formation' in D. Halperin, ed., *Psychodynamic Perspectives on Religion, Sect and Cult* (Boston, Mass., John Wright PGSC Inc., 1983), pp. 257–66.

Harrison, Harry, *Great Balls of Fire! A History of Sex in Science Fiction.* Grosset and Dunlap, 1977.

Hartwell, David, *Age of Wonders: Exploring the World of Science Fiction.* New York, Walker, 1984.

Herbert, Frank, ed. Tim O'Reilly, *The Maker of Dune: Insights of a Master of Science Fiction.* New York, Berkley, 1987.

*Hillegas, M. R., *The Future as Nightmare: H.G.Wells and the Anti-Utopians.* Carbondale, Southern Illinois University Press, 1974.

Holdstock, Robert and Edwards, Malcolm, *Alien Landscapes.* New York, Mayflower Books, 1979.

Huntington, John, *Critical Essays on H.G. Wells.* Boston, Mass., G. K. Hall, 1991.

*James, Edward, *Science Fiction in the Twentieth Century.* Oxford, Oxford University Press, 1994.

Jakubowski, Maxim and James, Edward, eds., *The Profession of Science Fiction.* Houndmills, Basingstoke, Macmillan, 1992.

Johnson, Wayne L., *Ray Bradbury*. New York, Frederick Ungar, 1980.

Ketterer, David, *Canadian Science Fiction and Fantasy*. Bloomington, Ind., Indiana Univiversity Press, 1992.

Ketterer, David, *Imprisoned in a Tesseract: the Life & Work of James Blish*. Kent, Ohio, Kent State University Press, 1987.

Ketterer, David, *New Worlds for Old: the Apocalyptic Imagination, Science Fiction and American Literature*. Bloomington, Ind., Indiana University Press, 1974.

Knight, Damon, *In Search of Wonder: Essays on Modern Science Fiction*, 2nd. edn. Chicago, Advent, 1967.

Kreuziger, Frederick A., *The Religion of Science Fiction*. Bowling Green, Ohio, Bowling Green State University Popular Press, 1986.

Lambourne, Robert, Shallis, Michael and Shortland, Michael, *Close Encounters? Science and Science Fiction*. Bristol, Adam Hilger, 1990.

Le Guin, Ursula K., *The Language of the Night: Essays on Fantasy and Science Fiction*. London, Women's Press, 1989.

Lem, Stanislaw, *Microworlds: Writing on Science Fiction and Fantasy*. London, Mandarin, 1991.

*Lewis, C. S., *Of Other Worlds: Essays and Stories*. London, Geoffrey Bles, 1966.

Lewis, C. S., *Of This and Other Worlds: Essays and Stories*. London, Collins, 1982.

Mackey, Douglas A., *Philip K. Dick*. Boston, Mass., G. K. Hall, 1988.

Mackey, Douglas A., 'Science Fiction and Gnosticism' (*Missouri Review* 7.2, February 1984, pp. 112–20).

Malik, Rex, ed., *Future Imperfect: Science Fact and Science Fiction*. London: Francis Porter, 1980.

Malmgren, Carl D., *Worlds Apart: Narratology of Science Fiction*. Bloomington, Ind., Indiana University Press, 1991.

Manlove, C. N., *Christian Fantasy*. London, Macmillan, 1992.

*Manlove, C. N., *Science Fiction: Ten Explorations*. London, Macmillan, 1986.

Martin, Graham, 'SF' in *Science, Technology and Popular Culture*. Milton Keynes, Open University Press, 1982.

May, Stephen, 'Salvation, Culture and Science Fiction', in T. Hart, and D. Thimell, eds., *Christ in our Place* (Exeter, Paternoster, 1989), pp. 329–44.

McHale, Brian, *Postmodernist Fiction*. New York, Methuen, 1987.

Mogen, David, *Ray Bradbury*. Boston, Mass., G. K. Hall, 1986.

Moskowitz, Sam, *Explorers of the Infinite: Shapers of Science Fiction*. Westport, Conn., Hyperion, 1963.

Moskowitz, Sam, *Seekers of Tomorrow: Masters of Modern Science Fiction*. Westport, Conn., Hyperion, 1966.

Moylan, Tom, *Demand the Impossible: Science Fiction and the Utopian Imagination.* New York, Methuen, 1987.

Murphy, Carol, 'The Theology of Science Fiction' (*Approach* 23, Spring 1957, pp. 2–7).

Myers, Robert E., ed., *The Intersection of Science Fiction and Philosophy: Critical Studies.* Westport, Conn, Greenwood Press, 1983.

Nemecek, Larry, *The Star Trek: The Next Generation Companion.* New York, Pocket, 1995.

*Nicholls, Peter, ed., *Science Fiction at Large.* London, Gollancz, 1976.

*Nicholls, Peter, ed., with contributions from D. Langford and B. Stableford, *The Science in Science Fiction.* London, Michael Joseph, 1982.

Nicholls, Stan, ed., *Wordsmiths of Wonder: Fifty Interviews with Writers of the Fantastic.* London, Orbit, 1993.

Nimoy, Leonard, *I am not Spock.* New York, Ballantine, 1975.

Olander, Joseph D. and Greenberg, Martin H., eds., *Isaac Asimov.* New York, Taplinger, 1977.

Olander, Joseph D. and Greenberg, Martin H., eds., *Ursula K. Le Guin.* New York, Taplinger, 1979.

*Parrinder, Patrick, ed., *Science Fiction: A Critical Guide.* London, Longman, 1979.

Patrouch, Joseph E. Jnr, *The Science Fiction of Isaac Asimov.* London, Dennis Dobson, 1974.

Pavel, Thomas C. *Fictional Worlds.* Cambridge, Mass.: Harvard University Press, 1986.

Philmus, Robert M., *Into the Unknown – The Evolution of Science Fiction from Francis Godwin to H. G. Wells.* Berkeley and Los Angeles, Calif., University of California Press, 1970.

Platt, C., *Dream Makers: Science Fiction and Fantasy Writers at Work.* London, Xanadu, 1987.

*Pierce, John J., *When World Views Collide: a Study in Imagination and Evolution.* Westport, Conn.: Greenwood Press, 1989.

*Pierce, John, T., *Great Themes of Science Fiction: a Study in Imagination and Evolution.* New York, Greenwood Press, 1987.

Pollock, Dale, *Skywalking: the Life and Films of George Lucas.* New York, Harmony, 1983.

Reichardt, Jasia, *Robots: Fact, Fiction + Prediction.* London, Thames and Hudson, 1978.

*Reilly, Robert, ed., *The Transcendent Adventure: Studies of Religion in Science Fiction/Fantasy.* Westport, Conn., Greenwood Press, 1985.

Rose, Lois and Stephen, *The Shattered Ring – Science Fiction and the Quest for Meaning.* Richmond, Virg., John Knox Press, 1970.

Rose, Mark, ed., *Science Fiction: a Collection of Critical Essays.* Englewood Cliffs, New Jersey, Prentice Hall, 1976.

*Rose, Mark, *Alien Encounters: Anatomy of Science Fiction*. Cambridge, Mass., Harvard University Press, 1981.

Rothfork, John, 'Science Fiction as a Religious Guide to the New Age' (*Kansas Quarterly* 10, Fall 1978, pp. 57–66).

Rottensteiner, Franz, *The Science Fiction Book: an Illustrated History*. London, Thames and Hudson, 1975.

Sackett, Susan, *Star Trek Speaks*. London: Futura, 1979.

Sammons, Martha C. '*A Better Country': the Worlds of Religious Fantasy and Science Fiction*. New York, Greenwood Press, 1988.

Scholes, Robert, *Structural Fabulation: an Essay on Fiction of the Future*. Notre Dame, Ind., University of Notre Dame Press, 1975.

*Scholes, Robert and Rabkin, Eric S., *Science Fiction: History, Science, Vision*. London, Oxford University Press, 1977.

Selley, April, '"I have been, and ever shall be, your friend": *Star Trek, The Deerslayer* and the American romance' (*Journal of Popular Culture* 20, Summer 1986, pp. 89–104).

Selley, April, 'Transcendentalism in *Star Trek: The Next Generation*' (*Journal of American Culture* 13, Spring 1990, pp. 31–4).

Shatner, William, *Star Trek Memories*. London, HarperCollins, 1993.

Shippey, Tom ed., *Fictional Space: Essays on Contemporary Science Fiction*. Oxford, Blackwell, 1991.

Shippey, Tom, ed., *The Oxford Book of Science Fiction Stories*. London, OUP, Book Club Associates, 1991.

Short, Robert, *The Gospel from Outer Space*. London, Collins, 1983.

Sladek, John, *The New Apocrypha: a Guide to Strange Sciences and Occult Beliefs*. London, Granada, 1978.

*Slusser, George E. and Rabkin, Eric S., eds., *Aliens: the Anthropology of Science Fiction*. Carbondale and Edwardsville, Ill., Southern Illinois University Press, 1987.

Slusser, George E. and Shippey, Tom, eds., *Fiction 2000: Cyberpunk and the Future of Narrative*. Athens, Ga., University of Georgia Press, 1992.

Slusser, George E., *Robert A. Heinlein: Stranger in his own Land*. San Bernardino, Calif., Borgo Press, 1976.

Slusser, George E., *The Classic Years of Robert A. Heinlein*. San Bernardino, Calif, Borgo Press, 1977.

Smith, Nicholas D., ed., *Philosophers look at Science Fiction*. Chicago, Nelson Hall, 1982.

Spivack, Charlotte, *Ursula K. Le Guin*. Boston, Mass., G. K. Hall, 1984.

Stableford, Brian, *Scientific Romance in Britain, 1890–1950*. London, Fourth Estate, 1985.

Stover, Leon, *Harry Harrison*. Boston, Mass., G. K. Hall, 1990.

Stover, Leon, *Robert A. Heinlein*. Boston, Mass., G. K. Hall, 1987.

Suvin, Darko, *Metamorphoses of Science Fiction: on the Poetics and*

History of a Literary Genre. New Haven, Conn., Yale University Press, 1979.

Tooponce, William F., *Frank Herbert.* Boston, Mass., G. K. Hall, 1988.

Vonnegut, Kurt Jnr, *Wampeters, Foma & Granfallows (Opinions).* London, Jonathan Cape, 1975.

Wagar, W. Warren, *Terminal Visions: the Literature of Last Things.* Bloomington, Ind., Indiana University Press, 1987.

Warrick, Patricia S., *Mind in Motion: the Fiction of Philip K. Dick.* Carbondale and Edwardsville, Ill., Southern Illinois University Press, 1987.

Warrick, Patricia S., *The Cybernetic Imagination in Science Fiction.* Cambridge, Mass., MIT Press, 1980.

Weedman, Jane B. *Women Worldwalkers: New Dimensions of Science Fiction and Fantasy.* Lubbock, Texas, Texas Technical Press, 1985.

White, Michael, *Isaac Asimov: the Unauthorised Life.* London, Millennium, 1994.

Williamson, Jack, *Wonder's Child: my Life in Science Fiction.* New York, Bluejay, 1984.

Wolfe, Gary K., ed., *Science Fiction Dialogues.* Chicago, Academy, 1982.

Wolfe, Gary K., *The Known and the Unknown: Studies in the Iconology of Science Fiction.* Kent, Ohio, Kent State University Press, 1979.

*Wollheim, Donald A., *The Universe Makers: Science Fiction Today.* New York, Harper, 1971.

Some other reading

Cornwell, John, ed., *Nature's Imagination: the Frontiers of Scientific Vision.* Oxford, Oxford University Press, 1995.

Foster, M. B., 'The Christian Doctrine of Creation and the Rise of Modern Science' (*Mind* 432, 1934, pp. 446–68).

Galvin, Ray, *The Peace of Christ in a Nuclear Age.* Auckland, G. W. Moore, 1983.

Grenz, Stanley J., *A primer on postmodernism*, Grand Rapids, 1996 (esp. ch 1 on *Star Trek*).

Hooykaas, R., *Religion and the Rise of Modern Science.* Grand Rapids, Mich., Eerdmans, 1978.

Jaki, Stanley, *Cosmos and Creator.* Edinburgh, Scottish Academic Press, 1980.

Jaki, Stanley, *Science and Creation.* Edinburgh, Scottish Academic Press, 1986.

Jaki, Stanley, *The Saviour of Science.* Edinburgh, Scottish Academic Press, 1990.

Midgley, Mary, *Science as Salvation: A Modern Myth and its Meaning.* London, Routledge, 1992.

Moltmann, Jürgen, 'What is "New" in Christianity: the Category *Novum* in Christian Theology' in *Religion, Revolution and the Future*, tr. M. D. Meeks (New York, Scribner, 1969), pp. 3–18.

Nebelsick, Harold, *Renaissance, Reformation and the Rise of Science.* Edinburgh, T. & T. Clark, 1992.

Sagan, Carl and Turco, Richard, *A Path where No Man Thought: Nuclear Winter and the End of the Arms Race.* London, Century, 1990.

Sullivan, Walter, *We Are Not Alone.* Harmondsworth, Penguin, 1964; rev. edn. 1970.

Tipler, Frank, *The Physics of Immortality: Modern Cosmology, God and the Resurrection of the Dead.* New York, Doubleday, 1995.

Torrance, T. F., *Divine and Contingent Order.* Oxford, Oxford University Press, 1981.

Whitehead, A. N., *Science and the Modern World.* New York, Free Press, 1969 (orig. 1925).

Index of authors and titles

Index of subjects

absurdism 111–13
alien, the; *see* other, otherness
aliens 37–8, 45, 90–5, 116–18

change 2, 31, 58, 115–16
Communism 43–4, 48, 129
cyberpunk 21, 46, 105–9

despair; *see* pessimism
disasters 30, 45, 48, 75–6, 129–31; *see also* nuclear war, nuclear disasters
dualism 70, 75

extra-sensory perception 45, 71–2

fabril vs pastoral literature 23–4
fantasy fiction 22–5
freedom 126–7
future, the; *see* prediction
futurum 121

Gnosticism 69–71, 78–82, 123
God: abandonment/absence of 29, 30, 33–6, 39; attributes 83; as Creator 95, 123, 124; as the Other 118–21; as Redeemer 119–24, 128; relation to 104, 132
Gothic literature 27–8, 31

Holy Spirit 126
hope; *see* optimism
horror fiction 32–3
humanity: Christian view 122–7; destiny 39, 84–7, 110–11 *see also* optimism; pessimism; divinised 82, 87–9; limits on 29–30, 86–7

idolatry 124–5
immortality 87–9
individualism 99–100, 104
infinity 86–7

Jesus Christ 65–6, 119–24, 128

loneliness 101–2

matter, repudiation of 73–6
mind–spirit identity 76–8
modernism 68, 109, 110

nature: power over 110–11; worship of 124–5
nuclear war, nuclear disasters 2, 5–6, 9–12, 29, 30, 45, 47–8, 128–9

optimism; *see* destiny; freedom; modernism; pessimism; progress; redemption; wonder
optimism and pessimism, ambiguity of 12, 30–1, 45–6, 127–31
other, otherness 15–16, 116–17; *see also* God, as the Other

personal identity 31–2, 36, 96–104
pessimism; *see* cyberpunk; disasters; loneliness; nuclear war, nuclear disasters; optimism; postmodernism
postmodernism 109–11
prediction 46–8, 120–1
progress 31

rationality, rationalism 27, 55–7
redemption: by aliens 93–4; by Jesus Christ 119–24
remembering 67–8
Romanticism 27–8, 31

science: and Christianity 34–6; and science fiction 130–1; *see also* prediction
science fiction: as adolescence 58–60; American vs British 18, 45–6, 60; in 'B' movies 11, 19–20, 29; as cognitive estrangement 42; as conceptual